Wildtrack Walks in West Dorset

Hugh Stoker

with sketch maps and photographs by the author

Mill House Publications
The Mill House, Seatown, Bridport, Dorset
Tel: 01297 489756

By the same author:

WEST DORSET WALKS
SOUTH DORSET WALKS
EAST DEVON WALKS
SEA FISHING IN DORSET
SEA FISHING IN HAMPSHIRE & ISLE OF WIGHT
SEA ANGLING WITH THE SPECIMEN HUNTERS
THE MODERN SEA ANGLER
A MANUAL OF SEA FISHING BAITS
COMPLETE GUIDE TO SEA FISHING
SEA ANGLING HOTSPOTS

First published 1996
Second impression (revised) 2004

ISBN 0 9508088 5 7

CONTENTS

IMPORTANT NOTE:
ORDNANCE SURVEY MAPS

Since publication of the previous edition of this book, the Ordnance Survey has introduced another type of 1:25000 map that is ideal for walkers. Known as the "Explorer" series, each sheet provides much wider coverage than the earlier "Pathfinder" maps listed individually in this book at the start of each walk. We therefore recommend the following:

Explorer sheet 116 for Walks 1, 2, 3, 4, 5 and 10;
Explorer sheet 117 for Walks 7, 8, 9; 12, 13 and 14
Explorer sheet OL15 for Walks 6 and 11.

"Pathfinder" maps can, of course, still be used by those readers who already possess them.

Introduction

WHEN I first published *West Dorset Walks* in 1982 I did so with some trepidation. Certainly I never thought that fourteen years and nine editions later many of my more energetic readers would, like Oliver Twist, be still asking for more.

So once again, in this little book, we will set out to explore the countless field and coastal paths, forest trails, bridleways, ancient drove roads, one-time smugglers' tracks and prehistoric ridgeways that go to make up West Dorset's unique network of public rights of way. As before, all the walks are circular, and have been selected to seek out the hidden places where you are most likely to encounter the timeless and unspoiled aspect of Dorset, and the wild creatures which inhabit it.

Where appropriate I mention the wildlife you may see on a walk, but needless to say it is the walker who travels quietly who will observe most. Indeed, very often it is when one pauses awhile, perhaps to eat lunch couched against the bole of a tree, that the most surprising encounters occur. For instance, there was that time when, while munching a wayside sandwich, a bluebell plant alongside me suddenly came to life, quivering and nodding vigorously, while all the others surrounding it remained motionless. Then I heard the sound of scrunching from somewhere below ground, and realised that a field mouse or some other hidden creature was enjoying a lunch of bluebell bulb.

All the routes described in this book are easily within the average walker's capabilities, but they *are* cross-country walks, and suitable footwear is therefore essential. The best choice for all seasons is a pair of sturdy, water-repellent walking boots with non-slip cleated soles - worn, of course, with thick woollen socks. However, on the upland walks in dry summer weather you may prefer to wear heavily cleated walking shoes. Smooth-soled shoes should be avoided at all costs; they are slippery on grass, and can be dangerous on the steep hill slopes and cliff paths of West Dorset.

Although sketch maps have been included in this book, a fairly large-scale Ordnance Survey map will prove useful and add to the interest of your walk. The best choice is one of the 1:25000 series, which show all public rights of way and field boundaries.

An inexpensive pocket compass will also prove very useful when exploring some of the more remote and seldom-used routes. The coastal walks are obviously well-trodden, and the paths clearly defined and waymarked. On many inland walks, however, there may be no visible path when crossing grassy fields and meadows - just the stiles and gateways linking each section of a right of way. On these "off-the-beaten-track" sections I have purposely made my directions more explicit, and where necessary have included simple compass bearings. These can be particularly useful when your next objective - be it stile, footbridge or gateway - happens to be hidden on the far side of a hill, or behind some overhanging tree branches.

Finally, do please observe the Country Code when sampling these walks. Don't park your car where it will obstruct a narrow lane or passing place, or prevent tractors and trailers manoeuvering into a field gateway. Don't pick wildflowers - leave them to bloom and seed, and so give pleasure to others in years to come. If you have a dog, keep it under close control at all times. Keep it on a lead when walking in sheep country, or near woodland game reserves. Happy wandering!

Walk No. 1

LAMBERT'S CASTLE AND BEYOND

Lambert's Castle car park - Bridewell - Roughmoor Cottage - Higher Stonebarrow Farm - Wootton Cross - Tempest's House - Sheepwash Farm - Peter's Gore - Lambert's Castle
Distance: Approx. 5½ miles
O.S. Map: Pathfinder 1316 (1:25000); or 193 (1:50000)

ALTHOUGH this very enjoyable wildtrack walk begins and ends in West Dorset, part of its circular route lies in Devon. It begins at the National Trust car park situated at the NW corner of Lambert's Castle Hill (Map reference 366988). Access to the car park lies up a short

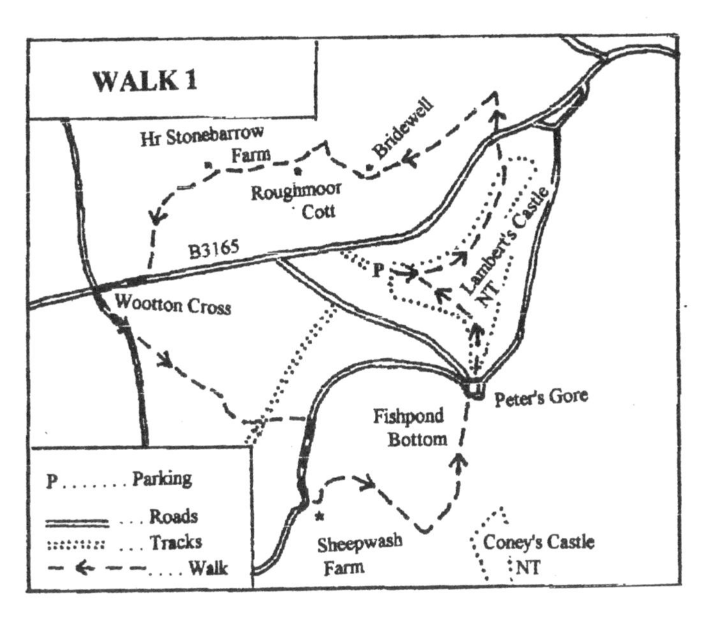

gravelly track on the S side of the B3165 Hunter's Lodge to Marshwood road. To locate it when driving from Hunter's Lodge, after about two miles look out for the "Fishponds" signpost. Continue past this signpost and turn right up the first gravel track beyond it.

From the car park you head E over a stile on to the wide, level expanse of the hilltop. Close to the stile you will see an information board which tells us that this was once the westernmost stronghold of the Iron Age Durotriges tribe. The defensive earth ramparts are not nearly so impressive as those to be seen at many of this tribe's other strongholds, such as Eggardon and Maiden Castle. (See *West Dorset Walks)*.

From the stile you head E, keeping a belt of woodland close on your left. Soon the path and neighbouring wood begin to curve around to your left, until you are heading in a roughly N direction. This eventually brings you to a gate leading into a hanging hillside wood of beech and pines. At this point the path passes through a single ditch and rampart of the ancient camp, although the earthworks are partly hidden by the surrounding trees. Here you are likely to lose all trace of the path under a carpet of fallen beech leaves, but your route lies downhill through the wood (very slightly W of N), and after passing through a gap in some bird-sown hollies you emerge on to the B3165. Cross the road, keeping a wary look-out for fast-moving traffic, and head for a footpath fingerpost almost directly opposite.

There is no visible sign of the path, but head down a pasture field, keeping the edge of a wood close on your right. Incidentally, on the day I made this walk, on a brilliantly sunny but frosty winter's morning, the low-lying country ahead was covered in a sea of mist, with isolated hill-top coppices and woodlands rising like small islands above the surface of the sun-gleaming vapour.

At the bottom of the field you join a bridleway. Turn left (SW) along this grassy track, which soon leads you into a wood. After a while this well-defined track rather surprisingly peters out into an overgrown area of ash and holly. On your left at this spot you will see a gate leading into a pasture field. Enter this field, turn right and head along the bottom edge of the field until you come to another gate which takes you out once again on to a continuation of the bridleway.

As you emerge from this second gate you will see on your right a deep, water-worn gully - which explains why this short section of the track has fallen into disuse. It also provides proof that the track must be very old, because it obviously existed before the gully cut across its course.

Soon after this the track skirts around the fringe of an isolated house called Bridewell and temporarily acquires a hard surface. Continue past the house and out through the five-barred entrance gate. Immediately beyond this gate the track forks. Take the right-hand fork (NW) and head downhill to the lower slopes of a very pleasant and secluded coombe. Before long this brings you to Roughmoor Cottage, and here the track passes a small wooden barn on your right. Continue straight on - ignore a field gate on your left and head W along a path which (at the time of writing) is almost concealed by encroaching bushes. This overgrown section only lasts for about 50 yards, and then it opens out again into a broader woodland track. On emerging from the wood, the track continues through some pasture fields and passes Higher Stonebarrow Farmhouse on your right. Here the track acquires a hard surface and continues up a short rise to a combined iron gate and cattle grid. DO NOT pass the iron gate, but instead pass through an unwaymarked wooden field gate immediately to the left. Follow a public footpath, keeping the field hedge close on your right. This eventually brings you back on to the B3165.

Turn right along this road for about 100 yards, and then turn left down a side lane signposted "Wootton". This lane used to be gated, and in fact a pair of white-painted wicket pedestrian gates still stand on either side of the lane, although no longer used.

Continue along this lane for about 80 paces and then pass through an iron field gate on your left. Although not waymarked, a public footpath runs from the gate in a SE direction to the edge of the wood at the far side of the field. On reaching the wood, turn left and follow the path along its edge, still heading SE. (If the field is down to hay or silage, walk around the perimeter - it doesn't add much to your distance).

The path (of which there is no visible trace) continues along the edge of the wood into two more fields. A little way into this third field the wood ends, and you come to a gate leading into another pasture field on your right. The footpath, although not waymarked, goes through this gate and heads SE, passing a conspicuous clump of pines on your right. Ahead you can just glimpse the roof of intriguingly named "Tempest's House".

At the far side of this field, near a small hay store built of waney-edged planks, you pass through a small gate on to a grassy track which skirts the grounds of the house. Turn left along this track, and soon you come out on to a lane.

Head straight across this lane (SE) and continue downhill along a narrow tree-flanked sunken way which, in winter, is carpeted with fallen beech leaves. After leaving the beech trees behind, follow the track around a sharp left-hand turn and then turn right when it joins a narrow and little-used tarred lane.

Follow this lane for about 250 yards until, on your left, you come to the entrance to Sheepwash Farm. In the hedge, at the left side of the entrance, you will see a "Bridleway" waymark post. Turn down this entrance track, keeping all the farm buildings on your right, and pass through a gate across the bridleway.

The bridleway now bears around to the right. Pass through a small wicket gate, which is usually propped open, and follow the narrow hedged track down into the bottom of a picturesque coombe, where you splash your way across a couple of shallow fords. By this time you will probably have recognised the track as an old drove. It was along this route, no doubt, that the flocks were driven to the sheepwash that originally gave the farm its name.

Heading up the far side of the coombe, you pass through an iron gate into a pasture field adjoining another farmhouse (Little Coombe Farm). Your right of way lies alongside the field hedge on your left, and then through an iron gate which leads you out on to a concrete access drive.

Turn right uphill along this drive until it joins another earth-surfaced bridleway at a T-junction. Turn left (NE) and follow this well-defined track uphill until you arrive at Peter's Gore - a place where five roads and two tracks meet around a grassy plot of ground. Here you continue almost due N to the far side of the intersection, and head up a gravelly track marked at its entrance with a National Trust sign.

This track takes you back on to the summit of

Lambert's Castle, a broad, grassy expanse of scattered gorse bushes and wind-stunted trees.

When you come to a spot where the track divides, take the left-hand fork which heads approximately NNW. This will soon bring you within sight of the stile leading back into the car park. However, if your visibility is reduced by one of the mists which often cover this hilltop, the above compass bearing will bring you back to the edge of the wood which covers the N flank of the hill. If you then turn left and follow the edge of the wood it will bring you back to the car park.

Points of Interest

Peter's Gore. In West Dorset the word "gore" is one that you will come across quite often in relation to places where three or more roads or tracks meet. Long ago, when the countryside in remote upland areas was still unenclosed, travellers approaching a crossroads and wishing to turn right or left, would almost invariably take a short cut. As a result a small plot of unused land would be formed at the intersection - triangular in the case of a three-legged cross, and diamond-shaped at a crossways. Such places would often be used by local cottagers to tether their goats, and we can hazard a guess that in the distant past this particular gore was used for this purpose by someone called Peter.

Walk No. 2

GOLDEN CAP AND A LOST VILLAGE

Langdon Woods car park - Golden Cap - St Gabriel's Water - St Gabriel's Chapel - Filcombe Farm - Langdon Woods car park

Distances: Approx. 5 miles starting from Langdon Woods as described below; or 6½ miles starting from Seatown. (See NOTE at end of directions).

O.S. Map: Pathfinder 1317 & 1316 (1:25000); or 193 (1:50000)

THIS walk offers a very enjoyable mixture of coastal and woodland scenery. It begins at the National Trust car park on wooded Langdon Hill. To reach it you turn S off the A35 on to a tarred lane by the short length of dual carriageway about 100 yards E of Frodsham service station, Morcombelake. Almost immediately after this

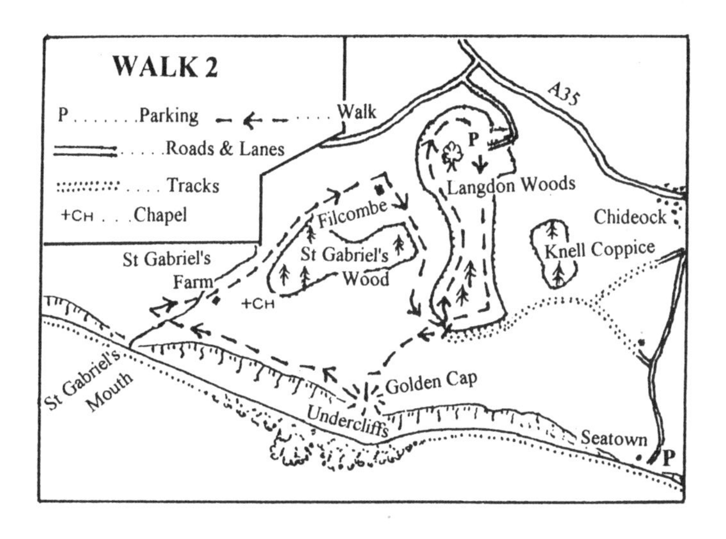

you turn left on to an unsurfaced lane; then after about 300 yards turn right up a forest road which ends at the parking area.

A broad contour track heads off from the N and S sides of the car park to encircle the hill. The dense woodland conceals an extensive badger sett, and other inhabitants include foxes, deer, grey squirrels and a variety of bird life.

Although the track is circular we will, for the purpose of these directions, set off by the S exit. This initial stretch is pleasant level walking, and through gaps in the trees you obtain magnificent views of the Chideock valley and its encircling amphitheatre of hills.

As you approach the seaward end of the hill the track curves around to the right and you enter Black Covert, a stand of mature pines. The ground rises steeply on the right-hand side of the track, and in several places deer and badgers have left well-worn tracks where they regularly scramble up and down the bank.

Before long the track makes another sharp right-hand bend, and at this spot you will see a side path which heads downhill for a few yards, and then forks to left and right. Take the left-hand path, which is signposted "Coast Path & Golden Cap". On reaching the bottom corner of the wood you turn right, passing through a gate into a grassy field. Head towards Golden Cap, and after crossing two stiles take the clearly signposted path to its summit. From here, if you have chosen a fine day, you will be treated to a breathtaking view of the Dorset and South Devon coastlines, from Portland Bill to Start Point.

The top of Golden Cap is almost flat, and from the Ordnance Survey beacon you head W along the grassy summit path, and then join up with a stepped path which descends the W side. You now follow the long distance

Coast Path, which takes you down into the bottom of the next valley. Here a footbridge crosses a small stream known as St Gabriel's Water.

After crossing the footbridge another path leads you up the far side of the valley into a pasture field. Here you turn right, keeping a hedge on your right. This soon brings you to two gates with stiles alongside them. Immediately beyond, you find yourself walking along a wide grassy strip of land which, according to local lore, was once the site of long lost Stanton St Gabriel. (See **Points of Interest).**

At the far left-hand end of this grassy area you pass a small thatched cottage, and a few yards beyond this you emerge on to a narrow lane which runs to left and right. To your right lies thatched St Gabriel's Farm, now owned by the National trust and converted into holiday cottages.

Just a few yards E of the farmhouse, up a bridleway track, you will find the ruins of St Gabriel's Chapel. (See **Points of Interest).**

After making a short diversion to view the ruins, retrace your steps to the spot where you previously emerged on to the farm's access lane. Here, on the E side of the lane, you turn off through a waymarked gateway, where a fingerpost indicates a grassy footpath leading to "Morcombelake and Langdon Hill".

Before long, by a delightful bluebell wood, you come to a fingerpost indicating where a side-path branches off to Morcombelake. Ignore this and continue straight on, passing a rush-fringed pool inhabited in season by newts, frogs and damsel flies.

Just beyond this pool you pass through another gate into the N fringe of St Gabriel's Wood. On your left the ground rises steeply to form a beech-covered knoll, and if you smell woodsmoke here it comes from the chimney of an isolated cottage hidden away among the trees on the knoll.

Passing through another gate on the far side of the wood, you continue up a grassy field to Filcombe Farm, keeping the hedge on your right. On emerging into the lane by the farm, turn right (SSE). A waymarked path leads you uphill across more fields to the SW corner of Langdon Wood, which covers the hillside on your left. Here you enter the wood along the same path that you left it by after the start of this walk. However, on rejoining the circular forestry track you turn left to complete the circle around Langdon Hill, and so back to the car park.

* * * * * * *

NOTE: This walk can also start and end at Seatown. From the Anchor Inn head W along the undercliff path to a flight of steps which takes you up on to the signposted Coast Path. Follow this clearly defined path to Golden Cap, where you then join up with the route described above.

Towards the end of the walk, on reaching the SW corner of Langdon Wood, DO NOT re-enter the wood, but continue straight on (E) along the bridleway which skirts the S edge of the wood. After 100 yards or so turn right over a stile and follow the signposted path back to Seatown.

Points of Interest

St Gabriel's Chapel. According to legend this chapel was built by a shipwrecked mariner as a thanks offering for having been washed ashore alive on St Gabriel's Beach. If there is any truth in the story, it must have happened a long time ago because the building dates from the 13th century.

Although very small, the chapel was probably adequate for the tiny scattered settlement of Stanton St Gabriel. In 1650, with its outlying farms and cottages, it supported 23 families, but some 150 years later the chapel fell into neglect and was used as a store for smuggled goods. It is known that remote St Gabriel's Beach was a favourite landing place for this purpose, and the track up the deep little valley of St Gabriel's Water would have provided a well concealed route inland to the chapel. An old photograph, taken during the latter half of the 19th century, shows that the building still had a thatched roof at that time.

Stanton St Gabriel. Often referred to as a "lost village", it was probably never much more than a small community surrounded by a number of scattered outlying farms - the main concentration being on and around the grassy area you traverse on this walk. It would seem that the "street" of this tiny hamlet ran along the west side of this grassy area, whilst some of the cottages backed on to the nearby stream. No visible trace of these dwellings remains, but here and there one can make out sunken strips of ground leading down to the now overgrown stream. My guess is that these grass-grown hollows were once the paths between the cottages, along which the occupants fetched water from the stream.

At the far end of the "street" there remains one solitary thatched cottage. It was probably the isolated situation of Stanton St Gabriel which eventually led to its demise - the final straw being when the old coach road over Stonebarrow* was replaced by a new road further inland.

* See *West Dorset Walks*.

Walk No. 3

HELL LANE AND EYPE DOWN

Seatown - Chideock - Martyr's Cross - Hell Lane - Eype Down - Thorncombe Beacon - Seatown
Distance: Approx. 5 miles
O.S. Map: Pathfinder 1317 (1:25000); or 193 (1:50000)

A CONVENIENT starting point for this walk is the car park immediately behind Seatown beach. Alternatively, in the out of season months, parking is

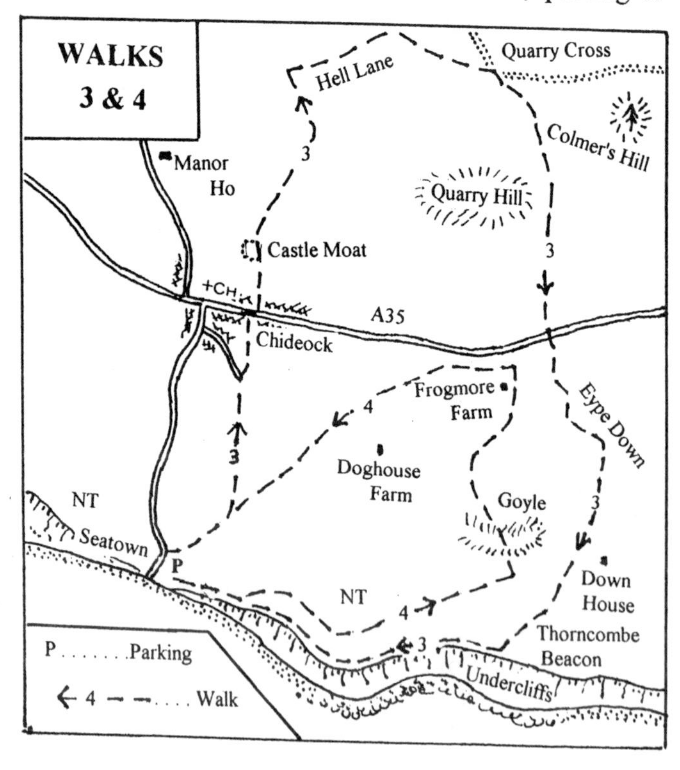

permitted (at the time of writing) along the E side of the road between the car park entrance and a point opposite the Anchor Inn.

Begin your walk by heading inland and forking right immediately beyond the car park entrance. This takes you on to concrete-surfaced Mill Lane. After about ½-mile, as you approach the outskirts of Chideock village, you fork right along a narrow footpath immediately alongside a cottage (Brook Cottage). Cross a small playing field and continue along another path which brings you out on to the main village street.

Cross the road and turn right, then almost immediately left up Ruins Lane. Halfway up this lane you will see a cottage with an interesting old leaden pump on your left.

Very soon the lane ends at a five-barred gate, which provides access on to a public footpath across an expanse of rough pasture known as Ruins Field. Continue straight on towards a large wooden cross, which stands on the hummocky grass-covered site of Chideock Castle, destroyed after it had seen considerable action during the Civil War. (See under **Points of Interest).** In the years following the end of the Civil War the tumbled masonry of the castle was used as a quarry to build many of the cottages in Chideock village, and today only the dry, rectangular moat remains.

From the castle site, head towards the top right-hand corner of the field where you will come to a stile. Bear right after crossing this and follow a clearly waymarked path, keeping the hedge on your right. After following the path around a couple of sharp bends, you find yourself walking along rising ground with a fine view on your left of Chideock manor house in the bottom of the valley, half-hidden among trees. Dominating the far side of the valley are the woods of Langdon - a very apt name meaning "the Long Hill".

Soon you cross two more stiles set close together, and continue alongside the hedge until it makes a sharp right-hand turn. Here, on a post set in the corner of the hedge, you will see a waymark indicating an intersection of footpaths. From this point you bear left towards the corner of a fence enclosing a group of withy trees. On rounding the corner of this fence you aim for a concrete cattle trough visible directly ahead. Immediately beyond this trough you cross a stile which takes you down into Hell Lane.

Turn right up this ancient hollow way, which climbs steadily until it brings you to Quarry Cross, where it joins another ancient ridge track. Turn right here (a fingerpost reads "Symondsbury"), but after only 40 yards or so fork right along another track which for part of its way becomes an impressive hollow way before eventually bringing you out on to the busy A35.

Cross the road to the tarred lane directly opposite, taking care when doing so because the visibility of approaching traffic is restricted. However, on reaching the lane do not carry on along it, but bear right up a narrow access drive alongside a cottage. Immediately beyond the cottage you come to a forking of tracks. Take the narrower left-hand path which takes you up a brackeny hillside on to Eype Down - an extensive and very pleasant stretch of common land. As you climb you get a grand view on your left of pine-capped Colmer's Hill, with Symondsbury village nestling under its eastern slopes.

This path takes you uphill in a generally SE direction. Ignore any side tracks which may wander off downhill on your left, and also the network of tracks which are made by deer, badgers and foxes. Eventually you should come to a fingerpost, and here you turn right and continue up a well-defined grassy track through the bracken and gorse. After breasting a rise and reaching what is virtually the highest point on Eype Down you will see immediately ahead, etched against the skyline, the summit of Thorncombe Beacon with its distinctive post and basket fire beacon. Incidentally, this is no ancient monument - it was erected in recent times to commemorate the 400th anniversary of the defeat of the Spanish Armada.

Follow the path down a dip and across a stile situated alongside an iron field gate. You have now left the common land behind, and after crossing the stile you continue towards the beacon, keeping the field hedge on your left. Before long you cross another stile, and close by, on your right, you will see a tumulus overgrown with gorse and brambles. The ancient men of Dorset who sleep within it now have a colony of rabbits to keep them company

From the burial mound it is only a short distance to the summit of Thorncombe Beacon. On a clear day it is possible to gaze upon the entire coastline of Lyme Bay, from Portland Bill to Start Point. Inland, beyond the distant Exe estuary, can also be seen the tors of Dartmoor.

From the summit of Thorncombe Beacon you head W along the cliff-top coast path. This takes you very pleasantly along a well-trodden turf track over Doghouse Hill and along Ridge Cliff, before making the steepish descent back to your starting point at Seatown.

Points of Interest

Chideock Castle and Martyrs. Chideock Castle was built by Sir John de Chideocke in 1380. It saw a good deal of action during the Civil War, when it stood for the king. It was attacked on several occasions by the Roundheads, who held the town of Lyme, and under Captain Thomas Pine, in 1643, took it with some 50 prisoners. Subsequently it was re-taken by the Royalists, but in 1645 the castle was again taken by Cromwell's forces. This time 100 prisoners were captured, along with 30 horses and a stock of arms, ammunition and gunpowder. The fact is that the castle was vulnerable to cannon fire, which was directed at it from three sides. One battery was positioned in the nearby churchyard, and the story goes that one cannon was hoisted on to the roof of the church tower, and from this vantage point was able to direct a devastating fire. In the process the church suffered considerable damage, including that caused by return fire from the castle.

Later that same year Cromwell's forces destroyed the castle, and for the next century or more the fallen masonry was carted away and used to build or improve many of the cottages in the village.

Now all that remains is the moat and some turf-covered hummocks, whilst in the centre stands a large wooden cross, erected in memory of the Chideock Martyrs.

Prior to the Civil War the castle was owned by the Arundells, a notable Catholic family, and under their "protection" many inhabitants of Chideock village shared their faith and attended Mass within the castle walls. The risk of doing so was great, and between 1587 and 1642 no less than seven were arrested, condemned and suffered horrendous deaths. Three were priests, Thomas Pilchard, John Cornelius and Hugh Greene, and four were laymen, William Pike, a carpenter, Thomas Bosgrave, a relation of the Arundells, and John Carey and Patrick Salmon, both servants who were found guilty of assisting Father John Cornelius.

In the years immediately following World War II an annual church service used to be held in Ruins Field to the memory of these martyrs, with the congregation seated on the banks of the old castle moat. I am not sure why the custom eventually died out, but suspect the reason lay in the dilution of the old close-knit "family" atmosphere of the village with the arrival of ever-increasing numbers of incomers.

WALK NO. 4

THE HIDDEN GOYLE

Seatown - Ridge Cliffs - Doghouse Hill - Frogmore Farm - Doghouse Farm - Seatown
Distance: Approx. 3½ miles
O.S. Map: Pathfinder 1317 (1:25000); or 193 (1:50000)

THIS short walk visits a delightful wooded coombe that is rich in wildlife. Tucked away in a deep fold in the hills, less than ½-mile from the Coast Path, it goes unnoticed by the vast majority of walkers exploring this superb stretch of coastline. From the naturalist's point of view, the most rewarding time to make this walk is very early on a fine morning.

Starting from Seatown car park, head E up the steeply rising coast path for about ½-mile until you come to a stile with a five-barred gate alongside it. Cross this stile and continue towards a fingerpost which you will see about 50 yards directly ahead. One arm of this fingerpost reads: "Coast Path", and the other "Camp Site East Chideock". At this point you need to take care, because your route lies between these two paths, along a broad grassy track which runs roughly NNE alongside a combined hedge and wire fence on your left.

This track takes you around the lower N slopes of Doghouse Hill, where in summer it is not unusual to see a family of fox cubs playing among the scattered gorse thickets on the hillside above. Continue along this track for just over ½-mile until you come to a stile in the hedge on your left. Cross this and head down a steep grassy field, keeping a hedge on your left. This path soon leads you down into a deep, thickly wooded goyle. (See under

Points of Interest). This area is a haven for wildlife, and over the years I have regularly encountered foxes, badgers and roe deer, and one summer I even came upon a feral cat who had a family of kittens hidden away in a hollow tree.

A small footbridge leads you over the streamlet at the bottom of the goyle, and from here you pass through a gap in some gorse thickets and head NW until you come to a wire fence backed by a hedge which, after 50 years or more of neglect, has grown into a line of sizeable ash, hawthorns, blackthorns, elders, holly and wind-stunted oak, with here and there the occasional clump of dog roses. Turn right here and follow the line of this "hedge".

The path takes you across two fields until, at the bottom of a fairly steep dip, you cross a stile. About halfway up the far side of this dip you will see on your left another waymarked stile. Cross this and then immediately turn right through a gate into a narrow sunken way with over-arching trees, and banks covered with ferns and ground ivy.

This track brings you very shortly to Frogmore Farm, and the right of way lies straight ahead between the farmhouse on your left and some outbuildings on your right. Continue along the farm access road until, just before reaching the nearby A35, you turn left over a stile into a field. Head towards the far side of the field where it adjoins the A35 hedgerow, and cross a stile which has a fingerpost alongside it. Head diagonally across the next field in the direction indicated by the fingerpost arm (roughly SW). This will take you into another field where you continue SW alongside a hedge on your left until you come to the access track to Doghouse Farm.

Pass through a wicket gate on the opposite side of this farm track. This brings you into a grassy field. Head SW towards a combined gate and stile in the hedge on your left. After crossing this stile you head directly across another track on to a grassy path flanked by a line of young pine trees. This takes you around the perimeter fence of a small sewage works and then across a bridge over the tiny River Winniford. Immediately after crossing this bridge, turn left through a small wicket gate into a grassy field.

Follow the clearly defined path across this field on to concrete-surfaced Mill Lane. Turn left along this lane, which soon brings you back to Seatown.

Points of Interest

The Goyle. In many parts of Dorset, Somerset and East Devon the word "goyle" is still used to describe a deep coombe enclosed at its upper end by encircling hills from which a spring issues. In the Purbeck area of Dorset the word is spelt "gwyle", which would seem to indicate that its origins are very old. Lutton Gwyle, near the lost village of Tyneham, is one such example. Others are Foxhole Goyle and Liberty Goyle, near Melbury Osmond; also Beacon Goyle and Roncombe Goyle, both near Sidbury. (See *East Devon Walks)*.

Walk No. 5

SYMONDSBURY AREA

Symondsbury - Axen Farm - Bilshay Farm - Allington Hill - Symondsbury
Distance: Approx. 6½ miles, or 7½ miles when starting and ending from Park Road, Bridport
Pathfinder 1317 (1:25000); or 193 (1:50000)

THIS walk starts in the village of Symondsbury, which lies just N of the A35, between Bridport and Chideock. Park the car in the fairly wide lane which runs NW alongside the church. On leaving the car, continue up this lane which hereabouts is flanked by several interesting old dwellings. In particular, look out for a cottage on your left which has an arched entrance and a massive studded oak door that would not look out of place on a medieval castle.

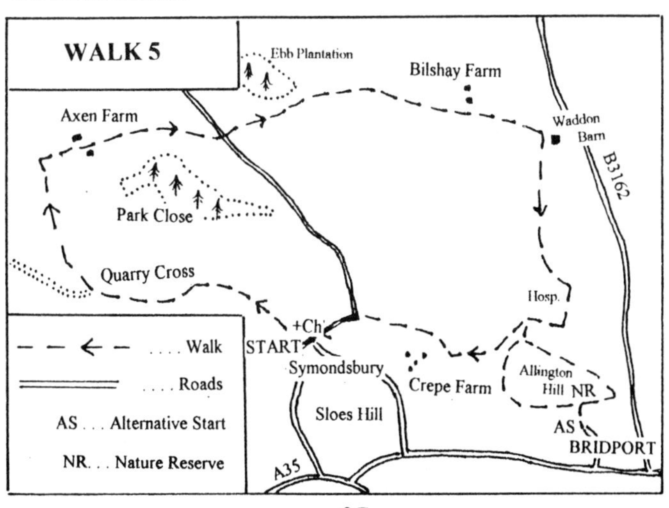

After just a few more yards the lane loses its tarred surface and begins to climb fairly steeply. For countless centuries this used to be a much-used drove road and packhorse trail providing access to the Dorset hinterland, and the constant erosion of scrabbling hooves has worn it into a hollow way flanked by over-arching hazels and steep banks covered in season with a cascade of wild flowers and hart's tongue fern. After a while these banks become progressively steeper, until eventually you find yourself in a miniature ravine with vertical walls of bare sandstone on either side. Bordering trees of ash, hazel, oak and holly filter out the sunshine, and their black roots protrude from fissures in the walls of golden rock on which generations of courting couples have carved their names.

On nearing the crest of the hill you emerge from the hollow way, and two "tributary" tracks join your route from the left. This spot is known as Quarry Cross, and is so-called from the ancient and now grass-grown quarry workings on top of nearby Quar Hill. At several places the sides of this hill have been deeply grooved by the horse-drawn sledges which, centuries ago, carried the stone down to the masons building Chideock castle, and the churches and dwellings of Symondsbury and Chideock.

Ignoring these side turnings, you press straight on along what now becomes a ridge-top trail, with expansive views opening up on either side. Below, on your left, lies the Chideock valley with pine-clad Langdon Hill beyond.

From Quarry Cross you follow this ridge track in a NW direction for about ½ mile; then branch off sharp right (NE) down a side track towards nearby Axen Farm. Unusually for this part of Dorset, the farmhouse is a comparatively modern chalet-bungalow, although the

A bluebell-fringed path near the edge of St. Gabriel's Wood. (Walk 2.)

Lucerne Lake, Melbury Park. (Walk 13.)

The ancient hollow way leading to Quarry Cross. (Walk 5.)

Powerstock village viewed from the bridleway described in Walk 8.

name "Axen" would seem to have an ancient ring to it.

Continuing straight on, the track leads you eventually on to the tarred Symondsbury to Broadoak road. Cross straight over this on to another cart track. This soon brings you into a grassy field, bordered on your left by a small wood called Ebb Plantation. The track, which continues close alongside a hedge on your right, now becomes concealed under a covering of turf, and in places is blocked by dense clumps of brambles and blackthorn. However, it is a simple matter to skirt these obstructions, until near the bottom end of the field the way ahead is blocked by a thicket of trees and undergrowth. DO NOT take the obvious diversion through the gap on your left; instead, bear right and climb over the rusty iron gate which lurks half-hidden by the overgrown hedge.

This leads you into a field which normally carries arable crops, so skirt around the curving edge in an E to SE direction. Very soon you arrive on the bank of the little River Simene, which is crossed hereabouts by a new wooden footbridge built alongside a tumbledown old stone bridge. Cross this bridge and head up the steep side of the valley towards a stile situated just to the right of the right-hand stone building at the top of the field.

Bear right after crossing the stile; then follow some iron railings which curve around to the left as they skirt the garden of Bilshay Farm. Soon the path brings you into another field, and from here you continue roughly ESE (there is now little or no sign of the footpath) until you come to a waymarked gate leading into another field. From here the right of way heads SE, and soon brings you to a waymarked stile. Do NOT cross this stile, which merely leads on to a short length of path providing access to the Bridport to Salwayash road. At the time of writing it also runs through an unoccupied chicken run!

From this stile your route heads almost due S, keeping a hedge and the buildings of New Close Farm on your left. Continue in this direction for about ½ mile, after which the path turns sharp left and soon enters an ancient hollow way. This track eventually brings you out alongside Bridport's new hospital, and here you turn right (W) and follow another old track which runs below the slopes of Allington Hill, rising steeply on your left.

Before long you come to a sharp right-hand bend in the track, and at this spot, on your left, you will see a notice board marking an access path on to Allington Hill. This notice informs you that the hill is managed by the Woodland Trust, and that walkers are welcome to enjoy its attractions. However, our route today lies up the main track which, as previously mentioned, takes a sharp bend to the right at this point. After about 100 yards you come to an iron gate across the track, with a wooden stile alongside, and immediately beyond this a side-track branches off sharply to the left, heading downhill towards the buildings of Crepe Farm in the valley below.

Just a few yards before you reach the lowest point of the track you will see an iron gate on your right leading into a field. Pass through this gate and then bear left towards the bank of a nearby stream. Follow this stream for a little way and then, just before reaching a small duck pond, cross a small footbridge - there is no handrail, so mind how you go! Bear right to continue along this ill-defined right of way, which heads NE and then ENE.

You will find yourself walking parallel with a hedge on your right, but it is inadvisable to walk too close to the hedge as the ground there is very soft and boggy. Keep to the rising ground, and soon you will come to a stile. Cross this and then bear slightly right and pass through a gate on to a path leading out on to a tarred lane. Turn left and very soon you will find yourself back at Symondsbury Church and your starting point.

NOTE: It is possible to start and end this circular walk just as conveniently from Park Road, which is situated at the West Allington side of Bridport. A gate at the top end of this dead-end road leads on to the E slopes of Allington Hill, and by following the track around to the N side of the hill it is possible to join up with the route described above, near the Woodland Trust's notice board. Similarly, you can end the walk by returning via Allington Hill, but this time following the circular track around the W and S sides of the hill to your starting point in Park Road. This is a short but very pleasant extension to the main walk.

Walk No. 6

A BUZZARD'S EYE VIEW OF WEST DORSET

West Bay - Wych - Bothenhampton - Shipton Gorge - Bonscombe - Walditch - Green Lane - West Bay
Distance: Approx. 9 miles, but see NOTE below for shorter alternatives.
O.S. Map: Pathfinder 1317 (1:25000); or 193 (1:50000).

THE very varied country covered by this walk can be guaranteed to provide a memorable day's ramble. Many readers, when they attempt it, will probably be surprised that terrain only two or three miles from the centre of Bridport should be capable of providing such enjoyable wildtrack walking.

NOTE: As you will see from the sketch map, the route of this walk takes the form of a modified figure 8 - the

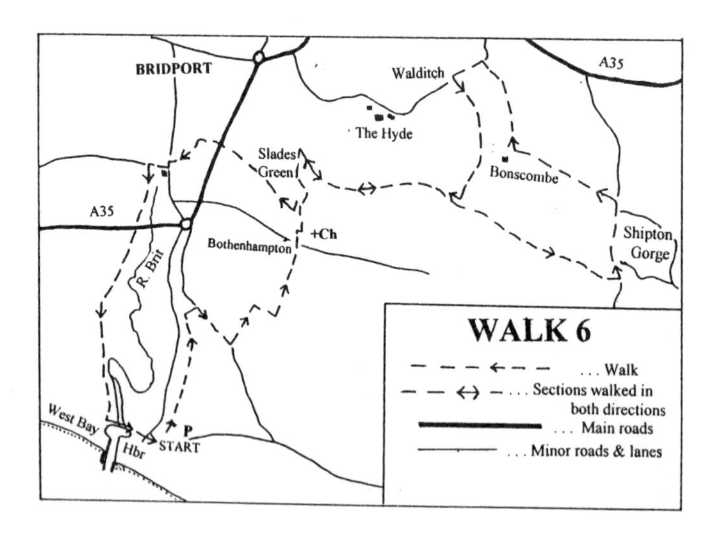

two loops of the 8 being connected by a short length of ridge track that is walked in both directions. Those readers who, through lack of time or energy, would prefer to split this route into two shorter walks can do so by tackling each individual loop of the 8. One loop, obviously, could begin and end at West Bay. The other, perhaps, at Shipton Gorge or Slades Green. In fairness to local residents, I do NOT recommend parking in Bothenhampton village, because parking there is both limited and congested.

* * * * * *

Your walk begins at the tiny disused railway station situated about 100 yards E of the harbour. After standing derelict for many years, the station was eventually restored with the help of Dorset railway enthusiasts. A public car park adjoins the station.

Head inland from the station along the disused railway track, which has now been given a firm gravel surface and classified as a path for walkers and cyclists. Before long the grassy fields on your right give way to a newly built (but imaginatively designed) housing estate. Cross a tarred estate road and continue along the path directly opposite.

Soon you begin to skirt the gardens of some older dwellings, and immediately after passing one with a lapboard fence you turn sharp right up a few steps on to a side-path. After just a few yards this brings you out on to the Burton Bradstock road. Turn right along the roadside footpath.

After about ¼-mile you will see a wide mown grass verge on the far side of the road, with a group of stone dwellings immediately beyond. Just before you reach these buildings you will see a fingerpost which reads: “Footpath to Bothenhampton ½-mile”. Follow this path up a private drive and then through a waymarked gate into a pasture field. Head straight up this field, keeping a wire fence on your right, and then through another gate at the top end. The path then takes you up a steep grassy bank on to a broader track which runs to your left and right. Either way will take you to Bothenhampton, but let us take the right-hand route.

The track takes you alongside a small stone-walled enclosure with a tall iron gate, and then past the end of a hedge. Immediately beyond the hedge you turn left down a field path which can become rather muddy after heavy rain. After passing the buildings of intriguingly named Marrowbone Farm on your right, you emerge through a gate on to a narrow lane. Turn left along this lane, which soon brings you out on to a somewhat broader lane. Bear left here, and then sharp right along a side lane (Old Church Lane). After just a few yards you will now see on your left a fingerpost which reads: "Footpath to Bottom Wood". Your route lies along this path, but before heading along it you may like to make a very short diversion to view Bothenhampton's old Holy Trinity church, which became redundant after a new church was built in the late 1880's at the other end of the village. Tucked away at the end of the lane, beneath an impressive ridge of the neighbouring downs, only the 14th century chancel and 15th century tower remain. The interior has been sparsely furnished to provide a small sanctuary. The oak reredos is perhaps the most noteworthy feature.

Returning to the fingerpost and footpath to Bottom Wood, you soon begin climbing steadily up a narrow sunken track which shows every sign of being as old as the village itself. You cross a couple of stone stiles.

NOTE: Readers opting for the shorter bottom loop of

the figure 8 route should turn left immediately beyond the second stone stile, which is approached by a short flight of stone steps. From here the route back to West Bay is described in the final paragraphs of these directions.

The route for the complete walk ignores this side path, and continues up a steep, brackeny hillside. On reaching the crest of the ridge you will come to a clearly defined grassy track running to your left and right. Your route for this walk lies to the right, but before taking it I would strongly advise you to head left for just a few yards to a grassy knoll where one is treated to a fine buzzard's-eye view of the entire Bridport area, with the rolling West Dorset countryside stretching away to embrace the iron age hill forts of Lambert's Castle, Pilsdon Pen and Lewesdon.

Immediately under the ridge, in a NE direction, are the extensive parklike grounds of the Hyde, one-time home of the Gundry family, whose association with Bridport's rope-making industry began in or about 1665, during the reign of Charles II..

Retracing your steps along the ridge track in a E direction, you soon come to a stile and gate on your left. Cross this stile and follow a well-defined path through another gate at the far side of the field. Continue along the left-hand edge of the next field and then, beyond the far hedge-end, into an arable field. Keep a stone wall on your left (almost hidden in places by small trees and shrubs). After only a few yards you will come to a waymarked stile on your left. Your path goes straight on, keeping the wall on your left, but pause at the stile and look down into the valley towards the Hyde. To the right of the house you will see a large stone building that looks a bit like a church. It is, in fact, a Real Tennis court - now restored after many years of ill-usage and dereliction. (See under **Points of Interest**).

Continue alongside the stone wall, and on reaching the corner of the field turn right along a rutted, grassy track, keeping a hedge of untrimmed thorn trees on your left until you come to an iron gate. Turn left through this gate and continue along a farm track. Ahead, and slightly to your left, you will see Shipton Hill - its unusual shape often being likened to an upturned boat.

After heading along this track for a couple of minutes or so, you will see on your left a picturesque coombe with a farmhouse nestling in the bottom. This is Bonscombe, and in due course your walk will be taking you, by a roundabout route, to the bottom of this valley.

Shortly after this you cross a stile, which brings you out into a green lane. Head straight on along this lane, and before long you join another lane at a T-junction. Turn left here (ENE) and eventually this brings you out on to a tarred road on the outskirts of Shipton Gorge village.

Turn left uphill, passing in turn the New Inn, a row of council houses and a side-turning on your left called Rockway. Finally, by a young tree growing in a triangle of grass, you turn left down a narrow hedged lane. Before long you will pass a timber bungalow on your right. Almost immediately after this turn right through a field gate waymarked with a blue bridleway arrow; then head down a short grassy slope towards a white-painted iron gate which leads you into a hollow way bordered by steep tree-grown banks.

Eventually this delightful track brings you out at the bottom of Bonscombe. Turn right now along a narrow lane flanked on either side by partly wooded hillsides which provide a favourite habitat for buzzards.

Turn left when this lane reaches a T-junction. This

takes you along a slightly wider lane into the outskirts of Walditch village. Very soon, on your left, you will see a fingerpost reading: "Footpath to Shipton Gorge 1½ miles". Take the indicated path, which begins as a grassy track running up between two cottages, and then begins to climb steeply through a dramatic tree-flanked hollow way. In places the banks on either side of this ancient hoof-excavated track rise as high as a two-storeyed house, and are covered with ground ivy, clumps of primroses, and ferns both fronded and hart's tongue. Here and there foxes and badgers have created their own mini sunken paths as, over centuries, they have crossed the lane and scrabbled up the steep banks on either side.

At the top of this sunken way you emerge into some pasture fields. From here you obtain a good view of some remarkable strip lynchets which flank the hillside a little to your right.

Continue uphill along the left-hand edge of the field. You pass through a pair of stone gateposts (minus gates) and almost immediately afterwards cross a stile. Here, on your right, you will see an exposed layer of rock where the local golden-hued stone was once quarried. The stone is so neatly broken up into horizontal and vertical joints, probably by the weather, that one could be excused for thinking at first glance that it was a man-made wall.

The grassy track now runs alongside an arable field and then through a gap in a hedge into another field. This brings you back on to your outgoing route, and here you turn right and retrace your steps to the stone stile with steps leading up to it.

However, this time you do not cross the stile. Instead, you turn right along a narrow blackthorn-fringed path which soon broadens out into a track known as Green Lane, and then acquires a tarred surface as it passes through a small housing estate known as Slades's Green.

A footpath alongside the estate road takes you downhill to another road (Crock Lane). Cross the road and continue down the fingerposted footpath directly opposite.

This path brings you to Sea Road South, which was constructed some years ago on the disused railway track that you set out along at the start of this walk. Wait for a gap in the traffic and cross the road to a clearly defined footpath which crosses some meadows and, skirting the N side of a Safeways car park, brings you out on to another road near Bridport's brewery - notable for the fact that it possesses a massive expanse of thatched roof.

Head towards the brewery, which is on the opposite side of the road, and turn right by the traffic lights. This very soon brings you to a bridge over the River Brit. On the far side of the bridge you turn left on to a fingerposted riverside path. Look out for the massive waterwheel at the rear of the brewery.

Before long the path veers away from the river and takes you past an isolated pink-washed thatched cottage; then passes under a bridge carrying the A35. From here it is a very pleasant, easy level walk across a series of meadows to your starting point at West Bay.

Points of Interest

The Real Tennis Court at the Hyde. Close to the Hyde, one-time home of the Gundry family, stands a Real Tennis court with a somewhat chequered history. Used as a hangar for tanks by the US Army during WWII, and then allowed to fall derelict for many years, it has now been restored to its original use. Very few similar courts remain for this ancient game that was once played by Henry VIII.

Walk No. 7

EGGARDON HILL FORT AND KING JOHN'S CASTLE

Eggardon Hill - Castle Hill - Nettlecombe - Knowle Hill - Spyway Inn - South Eggardon Farm - North Eggardon Farm - Eggardon Hill
Distance: Approx. 8½ miles
O.S. Map: Pathfinder 1317 (1:25000); or 193 (1:50000)

THIS is a superb walk at any time of year, but to enjoy it to the full you should choose a fine day with good visibility.

To reach the starting point from Bridport, take the A35 towards Dorchester, but about 2 miles out of Bridport turn off to the left on to a by-road signed "Askerswell & Maiden Newton". Soon the road takes you past the Spyway Inn, and then climbs steeply up the western flank of Eggardon Hill. As the gradient eases off on approaching the summit, some magnificent views open up on your left. Before long the road passes close to an Ordnance Survey trig beacon, and about 200 yards past this point you come to a cross-lanes. Here, alongside the right-hand turn-off, there is a parking space for two or three cars.

Opposite your parking spot you will see a narrow lane signposted: "Powerstock & West Milton - unfit for HGVs". Head along this lane for about 100 yards until you see on your left a hunting gate waymarked with a blue arrow. Pass through this gate and head diagonally to your right (SW) across a pasture field. This soon brings you to an iron hunting gate. Pass through this and turn right on to a footpath. Just a few yards further on you will be confronted by two stiles, set side by side on either side of a wire fence. Cross the right hand stile. Keeping the fence on your left, the path heads NW and takes you through the turf-covered ramparts of Eggardon's Iron Age hillfort. Although not so famous as Maiden Castle, near Dorchester, it is hardly less impressive.

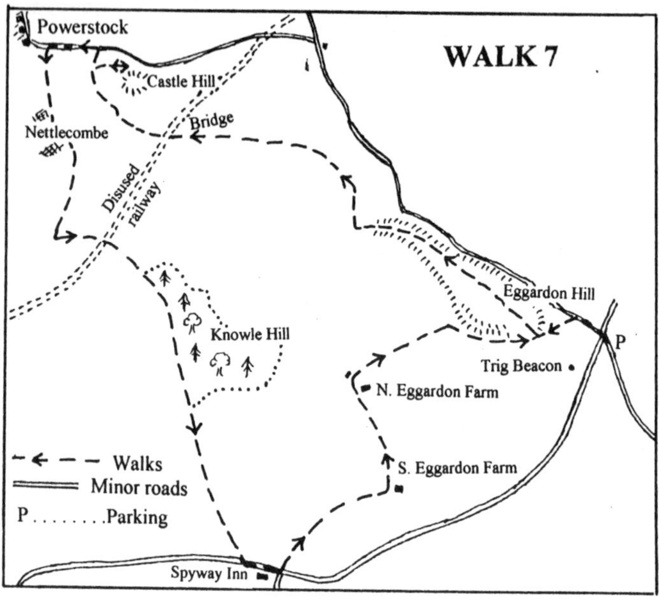

Continuing NW within the grassy confines of the fort, you are treated to some magnificent views of the rolling Dorset countryside. On your left, in the distance, you can see Thorncombe Beacon and Golden Cap, and to your right the extensive woodlands of Powerstock Forest. But perhaps the most eye-catching feature of all stands beside your path - in all that empty expanse of time-etched hilltop stands a solitary wind-warped thorn tree. It is the only tree on all that exposed hilltop that has managed to survive the elements.

As you emerge through the ramparts on the far side of the hillfort you lose the view on your right, but that on your left opens up, and you will see a small escarpment of white limestone protruding through the steep turfy flank of the hill ahead. Below it, amidst several other boulders half-hidden in the undergrowth, lies the Bell Stone, which you will see marked on the large-scale O.S. map. There is an ancient belief that in prehistoric times this large boulder was involved in some kind of religious rite, and the name may well derive from the god Baal (or Beal). If there is any truth in this belief, then the protruding strata of rock on the hillside would have made an excellent vantage point for the non-involved spectators.

As you continue along the top of this escarpment the top of Eggardon narrows like the prow of a ship, and begins to decrease gradually in height. After crossing a stile, continue along the "prow", and as the point of the hill becomes progressively narrower you may find the path becomes somewhat overgrown in places by out-reaching blackthorn branches. However, with a little perseverance you will soon come to a place on your right where it is a simple matter to leave the path and scramble down the flank of the hill.

At the foot of the hill you find yourself in a hummocky tract of rough grassland littered with numerous tumbled white boulders. It looks as if, long ago, the area may have been the site of a small quarry.

From here head due N until you meet up with a farm track. Turn left along this, and soon you will come to a fingerpost which bears the map reference: SY 531955. Take the path to Powerstock indicated by this fingerpost. Head up a short rise, crossing two stiles. Then continue straight on, keeping a hedge on your right.

When I walked this way, on a crisp, sunny December morning, I surprised a small group of roe deer feeding in the field on the far side of this hedge.

Before long you cross another stile, and this brings you on to an ivy-covered brick footbridge which crosses the now defunct Bridport to Maiden Newton railway track.

Continue straight on after crossing the bridge, until you come to a stile set in the hedge on your right. Cross this and follow the footpath which now descends a short length of picturesque wooded hillside, providing glimpses through the trees of Castle Mill Farm on your right. NOTE: At one point, where the footpath has slipped away, people have trodden a secondary path downhill towards the farm buildings. Ignore this, and instead scramble a yard or two higher up the bank to rejoin the true path, which soon brings you on to a tarred lane. Here you will see a fingerpost, and just a few yards from the fingerpost you cross a small stream by a wooden footbridge. This takes you on to a bridleway which, at its lower end, can become rather muddy in winter. However the going gets firmer as the track climbs up the W flank of Castle Hill.

Eventually the track begins to descend again, and here you turn off to the right along a path which soon brings you out on to the summit of Castle Hill. An area of grassy hollows, with here and there a course of dressed stone breaking through the turf, is all that remains of King John's Castle, which once lorded it over the villages of Powerstock and Nettlecombe, nestling beneath the hill.

Local tradition has it that, long before the castle was built, King Athelstan, grandson of Alfred the Great, chose this same site to build a hunting lodge, which was probably of timber construction. In those days it is likely that the forest came right up to the NE foot of the hill, and indeed even today only one farmstead (Whetley Farm) lies between your history-steeped viewpoint and the still extensive tract of Powerstock Forest. Roe and fallow deer still graze the forest and surrounding farm land, and it is interesting to think that they are probably directly descended from those herds which were once hunted by King Athelstan.

From the summit of Castle Hill you retrace your steps eastwards along the path until it rejoins the previously mentioned bridleway. Here you turn right and head downhill along what now becomes a tree-fringed hollow way.

Before long this track brings you out on to a narrow tarred lane. Turn left and follow this lane up a hill until it makes a sharp right-hand turn. Here, just before the commencement of the turn, you turn off to the left down a narrow footpath. The path is marked by a fingerpost which reads "Nettlecombe ¼-mile", but it is not immediately obvious as it is almost hidden in a hedge.

The path leads you down into the bottom of the valley, and takes you across a stream by a wooden footbridge and wicket gate. Bear slightly left across a rough pasture field and across another footbridge, and then through a hunting gate. The path then takes you uphill across some more rough grazing. The spoor of the path should be fairly obvious, but failing that head slightly to the right of a hedge on the skyline. At the top of this rise the path brings you out through a field gate on to a tarred road, and (very conveniently) immediately alongside the Marquess of Lorne public house.

Opposite the pub the road forks. Take the left-hand fork which soon brings you into Nettlecombe village. Here you turn right and head due S down a tarred lane for about 350 yards until you come to a junction, with tarred roads leading left and right, and an earth track continuing straight ahead. Follow this unsurfaced track until, after about 300 yards, it forks by a small plantation of conifers. Take the left fork, which very soon takes you back across the disused railway track.

From here the path continues in a roughly SSE direction, and then curves to the right around the bottom edge of a long belt of woodland shown as Knowle Hill on the 1:25000 map. At the far end of the wood the path brings you out into an open pasture field with a fluorescent orange post set beside the left-hand hedge marking the route of a gas pipeline.

From this point you head on down the field, keeping the hedge on your left and aiming for a gateway with a stile alongside it. Cross this stile and head on downhill, aiming now for a gateway about 40 yards to the right of a barn. After passing through this gateway you join a track which meanders in a generally SE direction and brings you out on to a tarred road near the Spyway Inn.

Turn left along the road, and about 75 yards beyond the inn you turn left again up the drive leading to South Eggardon Farm, which is classified as a bridleway. Shortly after passing some thatched cottages on your right you turn off to the left through a hunting gate fingerposted: "North Eggardon". Keeping a fence on your right, the path soon skirts the end of a picturesque lake.

From the lake a recently diverted section of the path takes you diagonally across a grassy field to the far right-hand corner. From there, entering another pasture field, you head up to a waymarked five-barred gate, and then, a little way on, through a waymarked hunting gate into a grassy field. Follow a line of electricity poles up towards North Eggardon Farm. As you draw near the house you will see, on your left, a five-barred gate.

As you pass through this gate, spare a glance for the fine old Holm Oak which spreads its branches beside the farmhouse. Incidentally, North Eggardon Farm was once owned by Isaac Gulliver, the famous smuggler whose operations extended all along the Dorset coast and beyond. (See under **Points of Interest**).

Heading up from the farmhouse along a clearly waymarked bridleway, you circle around some farm buildings until you come to a fingerpost marked with the map reference SY 533942, and from there follow the track marked: "Bridleway to Eggardon Hill". For some considerable distance this takes you straight up the flank of Eggardon in an ENE direction, and for part of that stretch the track thrusts its way through two lines of scratchy blackthorn bushes.

Eventually, after a stiff climb, you pass through an iron hunting gate on to the lower ramparts of the hillfort. Here I suggest you pause to admire the magnificent view - and to regain your breath!

Looking back across the valley you see the Knoll Hill woodlands by which you came, and over the top of these woods, hazy in the distance, there are the sea-bordered heights of Thorncombe Beacon and, a little to the right, the distinctive flat-topped crest of Golden Cap.

After passing through the hunting gate, bear away to your right (SE) along a grassy path which follows the dip between the lower rampart of the hillfort and the slope of the hillside on your left. Eventually this brings you back to the twin stiles which you negotiated on the outward leg of your walk - only this time you are returning by the more southerly of the two stiles.

From here you turn left through the iron hunting gate and head ENE across the field to the final gate leading out on to the lane. Here you turn right to return to your parked car.

Points of Interest

Isaac Gulliver was undoubtedly the most successful smuggler of all time. He hailed from Kinson, near Poole, but profits from his "free-trading" activities enabled him to acquire properties and farms all over Dorset. Needless to say, they were strategically placed to facilitate the landing and storing of his cargoes, and the stabling of his numerous strings of pack ponies. One of these farms was North Eggardon, which included land extending to the summit of the hill. It became the headquarters for his western smuggling activities, and with an eye to the future that was typical of the man, he planted a small clump of conifers on top of the hill to provide a landmark for his crews. Today no trace of these trees remains on the exposed hilltop, but a low octagonal bank in the turf marks the enclosure that was originally raised to protect them.

The outstanding success of Isaac Gulliver, when compared with other smugglers of his time, was due in no small part to the fact that on one occasion he came into possession of information that enabled him to warn George III of a plot to assassinate him. In response, the grateful king let it be known that he would look with displeasure upon any over-zealous officials who attempted to hinder Gulliver's business activities.

The extent of these activities may be judged from the fact that he owned 15 fast luggers, and ran a small army of bodyguards who were also responsible for the handling and transportation overland of his contraband goods. He is reputed to have been a model employer, and saw to it that they were all smartly dressed. He also issued them with hair powder, which was fashionable in those days. This earned them the title of "White Wigs" among other smugglers.

Towards the end of his life he lived in Wimborne, and by that time he owned properties in Dorset, Hampshire, Somerset and Wiltshire. He died at the age of 77, and was buried at Wimborne Minster.

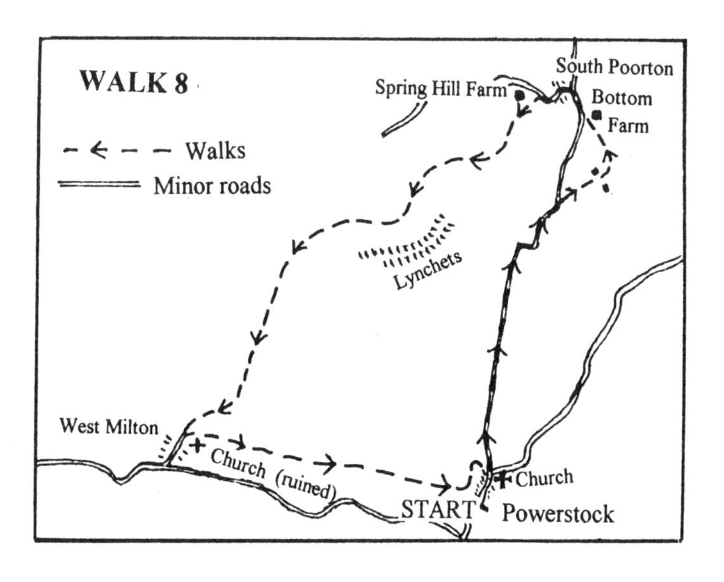

Walk No. 8

BY HOLLOW WAY AND LONELY VALLEY

Powerstock - Spring Hill Farm - West Milton - Powerstock
Distance: Approx. 5 miles
O.S. Map: Pathfinder 1317 (1:25000); or 194 (1:50000)
NOTE: See also sketch map on previous page.

THIS interesting and varied wildtrack walk will provide you with a "traveller's sample" of the unspoilt West Dorset hinterland at its best. It begins in Powerstock village. Head up the village street towards the church (see under **Points of Interest**) where five roads meet. Three of these are signposted, and of the two which are not, one heads downhill and the other heads N gently uphill. Take the uphill lane and continue along it until you come to a fork.

Take the right-hand fork along a narrow uphill lane, which for much of its length is carpeted along its middle with a broad strip of grass and moss.

After reaching the crest of the hill, the lane begins to descend between high banks, and at the bottom of a very steep stretch you will see a lane branching off to the right and signposted "Poorton Hill Farm". Head up this lane. It passes alongside some tall trees which, in spring, are clamorous with nest-building rooks.

Soon the tarmac surface ends near a large house on your left, and here a grassy continuation of the lane leads straight ahead to a field gate. Pass through this gate into a small pasture field. A right of way runs alongside the hedge on your left and very soon takes you through another gate into a larger pasture field. Turn left and follow the hedge on your left until, after about 100 yards, you come to a stile.

Cross this stile and head diagonally towards a farmhouse visible just to the right of an electricity pole. This farmhouse, incidentally, is a fair distance away on the far side of a small valley. Soon you come to the edge of a very steep grassy slope which enables you to look down into the bottom of the valley. To your right you will see a thatched farmhouse (Bottom Farm). Pick your way down the slope, heading roughly NNW, and with the farmhouse garden close on your right, pass through two gates on to a lane. Incidentally, in the garden of this farmhouse I was intrigued to see what at first sight appeared to be a thatched dog kennel, but which may have been the up-market dwelling of some ducks which were splashing around in a nearby stream.

On reaching the lane, turn right and head uphill until you come to a somewhat wider lane. Turn left here and after about 300 yards or so you will see, alongside the gate to Springhill Farm, a waymarked stile. Cross this and head down a bank on to the footpath, which has been badly eroded with water from the spring which gives the farm its name. This soon brings you on to a broad sunken track beneath high, over-arching hazels. At first, especially in winter, the track is virtually a shallow stream, but a little further on the water has been piped, and the going underfoot becomes drier.

At the lower end of this track you will come to an iron gate. Pass through this and continue along the path until it brings you to the foot of a steep grass and bracken-covered hillside. The path now becomes slightly less obvious, but continue WSW along the foot of this bank towards a thicket of brambles and gorse, keeping the hillside on your right, and a steep drop-away into a wooded valley on your left. Eventually you emerge through a gap in a hedge, and then veer slightly to the left across another small rough pasture towards a stile at the bottom left-hand corner. Incidentally, I have often surprised roe deer grazing in this area.

After crossing the stile, turn left and continue along the line of the valley, keeping a fence and hedge close on your left. Cross another field and continue along the flank of the gently curving valley. On the far side of the valley a series of lynchets, some covered with bracken, provides testimony to the fact that these hidden hills were cultivated more assiduously in the days of oxen-drawn ploughs than they are today.

Hereabouts you will come to a short length of rough bramble hedge. Keep to the left side of this hedge, and after only 100 yards or so you come to another stile. This takes you into another sloping pasture field, and looking due W you will see a gate set in an overgrown hedge of blackthorns and hazels. Head towards this, making a slight diversion to keep to the contour of the hillside. The path now burrows through the blackthorn hedge and brings you on to a very brackeny hillside. The path through the bracken is clearly visible, and soon brings you to yet another overgrown hedge, where you cross another stile.

Continue along the valley side, which gradually curves around until, towards the end of this stretch, you are heading slightly W of S. After crossing another stile, head SW towards the far right-hand corner of the field. This brings you to a five-barred gate with a stile alongside it. Cross this stile, and through a nearby gate on to a bridleway, where you turn left. Pass through an aluminium-painted iron gate alongside a farmhouse, and so out on to a tarred lane.

Turn left down this lane, and after about 30 yards, just beyond a large yew tree, turn left again up a path and some steps into a disused but lovingly maintained churchyard. On your right you will see a stone tower - all that remains of West Milton's old church of St Mary Magdalene.

Continue towards a stile at the far end of the churchyard, where the branch of an ancient yew tree frames a fine view of distant Eggardon and the massive turf-swathed ramparts of its Iron Age hillfort.

Be careful immediately after crossing the stile because the ground becomes very soft and boggy due to what would appear to be the soakaway from a septic tank.

Skirt this soft area and head ESE across the field towards a partly-hidden footbridge. Beyond this bridge you continue along a path which passes a house on your right and then through a wooden field gate with vertical metal bars set close together to prevent small lambs from squeezing through. It is an old design, once common in Dorset sheep country, but not often encountered these days.

Still heading slightly S of E, you continue along the flank of a grassy hillside with a talkative stream hurrying through the valley bottom on your right. Eventually you come to a hunting gate giving access on to a broad track hedged on either side by over-arching hazels. Follow this ancient way until, shortly after it makes a sharp turn to the left, you find yourself looking down upon the roof-tops of Powerstock village through gaps in the hedge.

Continue through an iron gate and follow the path for a few more yards down to a broader lane. Turn right towards the church, and on reaching the village street head back to your parked car.

Points of Interest

Powerstock Church. Overlooking the village on rising ground, this fine old church is well worth a visit. It possesses a magnificent Norman chancel arch, with patterned capitals and pillars. The main south doorway (inside the porch), dating from the 15th century, also has some interesting features. Carved into the stonework on one side there is a king holding a book, and on the other side his queen is offering loaves of bread. Clinging to her skirts are two small children. Both king and queen are positioned immediately above some lesser mortals, and appear to be standing on the heads of these "underlings" - an interesting example of medieval symbolism which seems to indicate the stone carver may have lived during the reign of a despotic monarch who also had an interest in learning (hence the book in the king's hand).

Could it, one wonders, have been Edward IV (1442-1483)? He was certainly tyrranic in rule, but also a patron of new discoveries - including Caxton's invention of printing. If so, one of those children at the queen's skirts could have been the ill-fated Edward V who, at the age of thirteen, became king for just a few weeks upon his father's death. Then his uncle (Richard III), with feigned reluctance, accepted the crown for himself. Young Edward, together with his younger brother, were then murdered in the Tower by order of their uncle.

Close by, alongside the churchyard path, and pre-dating the doorway by some two hundred years, is what at first glance appears to be a time-worm altar tomb. It is, in fact, a very rare survival from the 13th century - a dole table from which bread was once distributed to the poor of the village.

Walk No. 9

A FOREST NATURE TRAIL

A circular waymarked walk in a 285 acre section of Powerstock Forest maintained by the Dorset Naturalist's Trust.
Distance: Approx. 3 miles
O.S. Map: Pathfinder 1317 (1:25000); or 193 (1:50000)

THIS walk begins at a small parking area at the NW corner of wooded Powerstock Common (Map Reference 547974). To reach this spot from Bridport, drive along the A35 towards Dorchester for about 2½ miles and then turn off left along a road signed: "Askerswell & Maiden Newton". Continue along this road past the Spyway Inn and over Eggardon Hill. Ignore two right turn-offs signposted Maiden Newton and Toller Porcorum. After

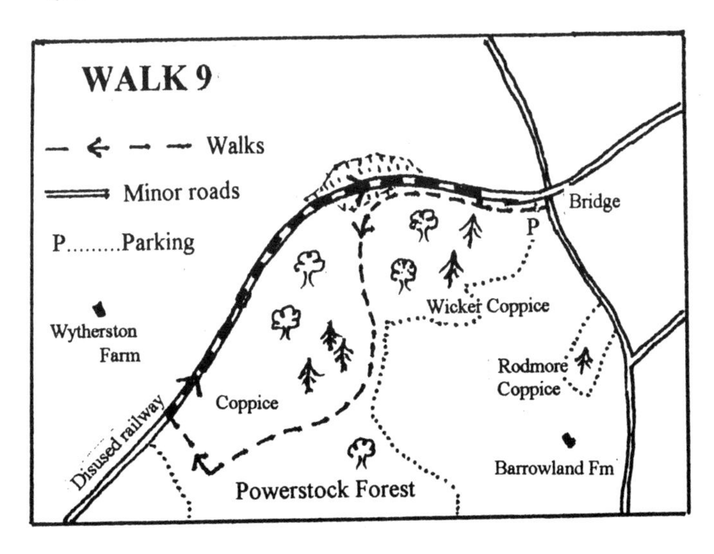

descending a long hill you will see the parking area on your left. A railway bridge a few yards further down the road will help you to pinpoint the spot.

From the parking area a bridleway heads W into the woods, and before long you pass a sign which reads: "Dorset Naturalist's Trust Nature Reserve. Please keep to the bridlepath. All dogs on leash". A little further on you arrive at an information board which provides illustrated details of the wildlife likely to be seen in the nature reserve.

At this information board you turn off to the right along a waymarked path. After just a few yards you will pass, on your right, a gate and stile which provides access to the old disused Bridport to Maiden Newton railway track. You will be returning by this route towards the end of your walk, but for the time-being continue straight on along the path.

Shortly after this you pass the first of several small ponds and pools which lie half-hidden among the trees. In summer they attract dragonflies and are inhabited by various small aquatic creatures, including all three species of newt.

The path also takes you past the remains of a Suffolk type brick kiln dating from 1857 - the same year that the adjacent railway first opened for traffic. Making use of local deposits of clay and sand, it produced roofing tiles and land drainage pipes in addition to its main output of bricks. The brick moulders normally worked a 14-hours day! An illustrated information board adjoining the site shows how the kiln looked when operating.

Before long the track divides, with a blue arrow pointing left and a red arrow pointing right. Follow the red arrow.

Picking its way through mixed woodland, the path

begins to head almost due S. Go straight across a broad forestry road on to a track waymarked with a blue bridleway arrow, still heading S. In winter parts of this path become quite muddy, and this offers a good opportunity to look for tracks of the local wildlife. When I walked this way in December there were numerous deer slots, and the unmistakeable broad paw prints of badgers.

Before long this path begins climbing on to elevated ground, with small scrubby oak trees on your left and an expanse of bracken-covered descending hillside on your right, beyond which is a fairly extensive plantation of conifers. Looking W above the tops of the conifers you have a grand view of the patchwork Dorset countryside, extending from the coastal heights of Thorncombe Beacon and Golden Cap inland to Lambert's Castle, Pilsdon Pen and Lewesdon.

At this stage of your walk you pass on your left a hunting gate waymarked with a blue bridleway arrow. This leads down to Barrowland Farm, but your route lies straight on along the E edge of the conifer wood. The path now begins to descend towards a large and neglected hazel coppice which has long passed its cut and sell-by date. However, it is a good place to go nutting in late September.

DO NOT follow the bridleway into the coppice, but instead bear right. After a few yards your path joins a broad forestry track, and here you head N. Before long this track joins up with another one, and here you turn left (roughly SW). Your route now begins to descend into an area of mature oaks, with rising ground on your left and low, almost boggy ground on your right, with the oak trees growing out of a ground cover of rushes and flags.

This track eventually ends abruptly in a small clearing, and looking ahead you will see a waymarked post carrying a red arrow pointing towards your right. Follow the indicated path in a NW direction, and soon you pass through a waymarked squeeze stile into an area of ancient oak woodland. Continue NW through the trees until you come to another waymark post with an arrow pointing diagonally to the right. Follow the direction indicated (almost due N) and this will bring you to some steps leading up on to the disused railway track.

Your return route lies to the right along this railway track, but first of all I would suggest you make a short diversion to the bridge which crosses the cutting a short distance to your left. On reaching the bridge it is possible to climb one of the paths leading up the side of the cutting on to the bridge. On the W side of the bridge you will see a small iron hunting gate. Pass through this into a pasture field, and climb the small grassy knoll which rises only a few yards away. From here you obtain a really fine view of the entire expanse of Powerstock Forest, whilst to the W, just beyond the far side of the field, you will see the buildings of ancient Wytherston Farm.

Returning to the bridge and descending into the bottom of the cutting you now head NE along the track, or to use railway terminology, in the "up" direction. On either side the track is bordered by untamed woodlands and rampant hazel coppices, and the old permanent way has become overgrown with a wide variety of plants. Many of these plants are chalk-loving and foreign to the area - encouraged to set up home here by the carboniferous limestone ballast used in the construction of the track.

Although the deer which inhabit the surrounding woods are shy, like most of their kind, many other wild creatures seem remarkably tame. While walking along this stretch of track a grey squirrel sat and watched my approach, and did not attempt to move until I was only two or three yards away. Then it casually lolloped ahead of me, making no attempt to gain the cover of the nearby undergrowth. Eventually, to my surprise, it disappeared through the half-open door of an old platelayer's hut.

A little way beyond this hut, where the flanking woods give way to steep embankments of rough tussock grass, you will see the well-worn tracks where deer have scrambled up and down the muddy slopes. It would seem that drainage must have been a problem here when the line was constructed, because you will pass two deep well-like shafts from which, in winter, there emerges the sound of rushing water.

Eventually the track ahead of you is crossed by a barbed wire fence, and just before you reach it you will see a gate and stile on your right. Cross this stile and turn left on to a path which soon brings you back to the information board that you passed on the outgoing leg of your walk. Turn left here and continue back to your starting point.

Points of Interest

Powerstock Forest is a large and ancient area of woodland, of which the DNT Nature Reserve forms just a small part. Tradition has it that King Athelstan, grandson of Alfred the Great, hunted here from his hill-top hunting lodge near Powerstock. There is also good reason to believe that King John, who reigned from 1199 to 1216, also hunted here when visiting the Norman castle which was built on the site of Athelstan's wooden hunting lodge

In 1957 the Forestry Commission began replacing the ancient deciduous woods with conifers, to the dismay of all nature lovers who cherished this rare and historic tract of unspoiled woodland. It was largely through the efforts of the late Kenneth Allsop, a well-known local naturalist and journalist, that a halt was eventually called to this undesirable programme of clearance and replanting.

Bridport Railway. The 9½-miles length of track between Maiden Newton and Bridport was opened for traffic in November 1857, but it was not until March 1884 that it was extended to Bridport Harbour. By that time the amount of shipping using the harbour was already declining.

I have fond memories of travelling between Maiden Newton and Bridport on this friendly little branch line - memories which date back to World War II when I was a serviceman heading back home on leave. On one bitter night in the notoriously cold winter of 1947, having missed the last passenger train at Maiden Newton, I was invited to travel in the brake van of a goods train that was on the point of leaving. Chatting cosily with the guard beside the van's glowing coal stove provided a memorable start to my Christmas leave - and at the same time fulfilled a boyhood ambition!

Walk No. 10

AIRMAN'S GRAVE AND WESSEX RIDGEWAY

Stoke Abbott - Netherbury - Parnham - Beaminster - Gerrard's Hill - Chart Knolle - Stoke Abbott
Distance: Approx. 7 miles
O.S. Maps: Pathfinder 1298 and 1317 (1:25000); or 193 (1:50000)

THIS walk begins by the church in the secluded village of Stoke Abbott. Two signs reading *12th Century Church* indicate two lanes leading to it. Take the more

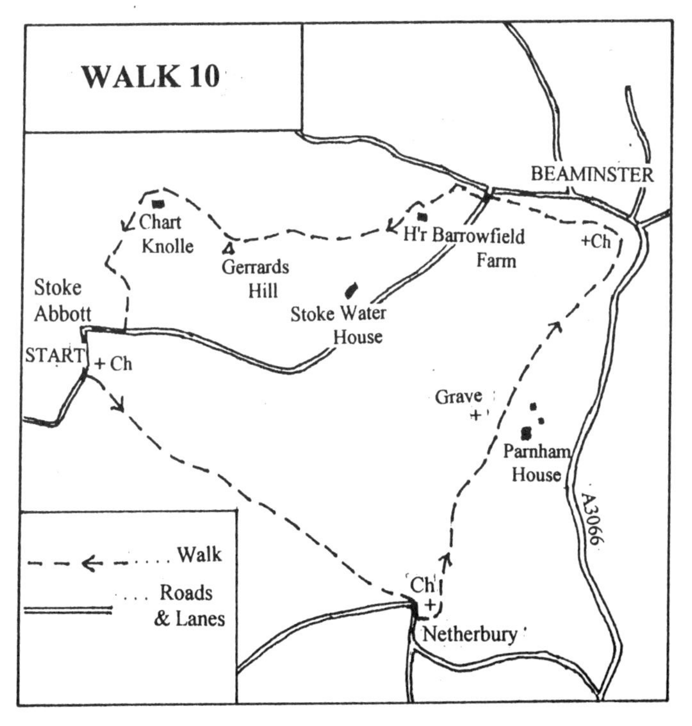

southerly lane, which soon brings you to the main gate leading up to the church. (See under **Points of Interest**).

Continue down the lane into a grassy field, then bear right (SE) past the gates of a small sewage works. This takes you into an adjoining pasture field. On entering this field, head diagonally to your right towards a hedge, where you will see a small green-painted gate. This leads you into a delightful uphill stretch of ancient hollow way, overarched with the branches of oaks, ash, sycamore, hazel, elder, blackthorn and the occasional rampant holly. There is even a yew - doubtless a bird-propagated offspring of the ancient yew in the nearby churchyard.

The banks of this hollow way are thickly cloaked in wild garlic, and when I walked this way they were just bursting into flower and filling the air with their scent.

Eventually the gradient eases off, and the sunken way opens out on to a grassy, tractor-rutted drove road. Here the wild garlic is replaced by hedgerow clumps of bluebells, primroses, scarlet campion, Stars of Bethlehem and Golden Archangels.

Your route for the next mile or so lies in a SE direction, so carry straight on along a minor track when the main track bears away to the left.

Before long you emerge into a large grassy field. Still heading SE, you descend gradually towards a belt of woodland in the bottom of a valley. Go through an iron gate, which brings you to a watersplash. After heavy rain it may be inadvisable to go through the ford, as the bottom appears to be deep silt. I elected to head upstream for two or three yards, where the banks narrowed and it was possible to leap across dryshod.

Go through another iron gate on the far side of the ford, and then turn left and follow the hedgeline to the corner of the field. Turn right here and continue along the hedge to a hunting gate. This leads you into a belt of very pleasant woodland with a clearly defined footpath.

On the far side of the wood you cross a stile and climb a steep hillside. At the top you pass through two hunting gates set close together. Still heading SE, you cross a grassy field keeping the hedge on your left. Soon you will come to a stile, and from this point on the footpath is clearly defined by waymarks and further stiles until Netherbury church tower comes into view.

When the path brings you out on to a lane, head downhill to the war memorial just below the church. Here you take a fingerposted footpath which leads you very pleasantly along a wooded valleyside above the River Brit. The stream, hurrying towards the sea at West Bay, is hidden by the trees, but in spring the distant roaring of a weir blends with the sound of birdsong.

Before long the trees thin out, and you come to a rusty dutch barn and the ivy-clad ruins of a house. Here you bear to the right and join a broad cart track until it curves away abruptly to the left. Here you carry straight on along a narrower waymarked bridleway which runs alongside the wooded perimeter of Parnham House gardens, glimpsed here and there beyond the trees.

Along this stretch of path you make a short diversion over a stile, which you will see on your left. Head up a steep grassy hillside dotted with trees until, at the summit, you arrive at an iron gate and railings enclosing the grave of Lieutenant William Barnard Rhodes-Moorhouse VC, of the Royal Flying Corps in World War I. He was the first airman ever to win the Victoria Cross. (See under **Points of Interest**).

When I visited this hilltop, with its extensive views of the surrounding countryside, it was a crisp but sunny morning in early April, and the grave enclosure was brightly nodding with flowering daffodils. The grave itself is thickly planted with a mass of wildflowers. Not many of these were in bloom so early in the season, but appropriately enough a few forget-me-nots were braving the chilly hilltop wind.

Returning down the hillside to the stile, you turn left and continue N along the path. Leaving Parnham House behind, the path crosses grassy fields and then broadens out into a lane as it enters the outskirts of Beaminster.

On entering the town you follow the road around gradually to the left until it brings you to the parish church, which you pass on your left. Continue along Shorts Lane which soon narrows to a bridleway before taking you over a stile into a small grassy field.

At the far end of this field you pass through a small gate and turn left along a tarred lane for a few yards, then turn right up a narrow lane. Incidentally, by now you will have noticed from the waymarks in this area that you are travelling along a section of the Wessex Ridgeway - a long-distance walk that explores 137 miles of countryside between Marlborough and Lyme Regis.

Continue along this lane until you see a factory car park on your left. Immediately prior to reaching this car park you will see a waymarked path on your left leading to a gateway into a pasture field. Head diagonally SW across this field towards the right-hand side of Higher Barrowfield Farm buildings, where you will come to another waymark. Bear left after reaching the corner of the buildings, but do NOT cross a white-painted stile on your left. Instead, head SW over the brow of a slight rise, when you will see a stile set in the hedge ahead.

After crossing this stile you head downhill across more fields until, at the bottom of the valley, you come to a footbridge across a small stream.

On the far side of the stream you head slightly N of W up a steep grassy slope towards a lone oak tree. (Do not be led astray by another path which wanders off to the left from the bridge). A waymark post is set alongside the oak, and I mention this because the roots of the tree (which looks as if it may have been struck by lightning) are badly rotted, and by the time you read this it may no longer be standing as a landmark!

Incidentally, while climbing this hillside you will see away on your left a large group of old buildings. This is Stoke Water House, a one-time workhouse which was held in dread by earlier generations living in this part of West Dorset.

From the lone tree you continue uphill in the same direction and pass through a gateway on to a farm track; then over a waymarked stile set in the hedge directly opposite. Head on W up a steeply rising field until you reach the highest point, which is marked by an O.S. trig beacon and a clump of beech trees. Known as Gerrard's Hill, it offers magnificent views of the surrounding country and distant sea beyond the West Bay gap. It was here I chose to eat my lunch, resting on a carpet of flowering celandines, and using one of the beech trees as a backrest.

There is a story that Charles II, fleeing with some loyal companions from Cromwell's troops after his defeat at Worcester, avoided his would-be captors patrolling the local roads and lanes by taking to this lonely hilltop route.. As I munched my sandwiches, I wondered whether that fugitive king had also paused on this vantage point to look for signs of pursuit in the countryside below. (See **Points of Interest**).

From the summit of Gerrard's Hill you descend in a NW direction along a clearly waymarked ridge track, and before long draw close to the quite impressive old house of Chart Knolle. A series of waymarked gates guides you around the right-hand side of some farm buildings and eventually brings you out on to a cart track.

Turn left along this track into what, for want of a better description, is the courtyard of the house. On your right is a building used as a garage; turn right after passing this and exit between a pair of stone pillars on to a tarred private road which is classified as a bridleway. Continue down this lane until you reach your starting point in Stoke Abbott village.

Points of Interest

Stoke Abbott Church dates from the 12th century, and the massive yew tree which stands beside it is probably as old. It is said to measure 18 feet around its trunk. Inside the church there is a font where children of the village have been baptised since Norman times. The font cover is an outstanding example of the blacksmith's craft. Near the font you will also see an array of staves. A notice tells us that these were used in an annual parade held by the Stoke Abbott Club on the first Friday of every June, until the custom ended in 1975.

The Airman's Grave. William Rhodes-Moorhouse was born in London in 1887. As a young man he developed a passion for motor racing until, a few years later, his interest turned to the new and even more dare-devil pursuit of flying. He took part in many air shows in Europe and America, and while competing at San Francisco he won the prestigious Harbor Prize. He was also the first aviator to fly beneath the Golden Gate Bridge.

Another of his "firsts" was flying the English Channel with two passengers, one of whom was his wife, Linda. They were on their honeymoon, and crashed on landing!

The track leading to Melbury Osmond. (Walk 13.)

St. Catherine's Chapel, near Abbotsbury. Note the turf-covered lynchets, carved out of the hillside by centuries of medieval ploughing. (Walk 11.)

The author admires the view from Girt Lane, near Evershot. (Walk 13.)
On a clear day one can see the mountains of Wales. *Photo: Don Foy.*

Looking out across the wooded countryside beyond Urless Farm. (Walk 14.)

Fortunately they all survived, but the experience was enough to make Linda beg her husband to give up flying. This he did until the outbreak of World War I, when almost inevitably he joined the Royal Flying Corps as a pilot. In 1915 he was posted to a squadron on the Western Front, at a time when the life expectancy of a combat pilot was measured in weeks, or even days, rather than months.

He had not been with the squadron long before he was given the solo mission of bombing a strategic railway line near Courtrai, in Belgium. This he accomplished, and in doing so prevented the Germans bringing up reinforcements by rail to the second battle of Ypres. However, to ensure success he had to attack at very low altitude, and was mortally wounded by ground fire. Determined to report the success of his mission, he managed to fly his damaged plane back through intense enemy machine gun fire, being hit again and again in the process. After making his report he was taken to a casualty station, and died next day holding a photograph of his young son, William Henry Rhodes-Moorhouse. For his "most conspicuous bravery" he was awarded the Victoria Cross - the first airman ever to earn this greatest of all military honours.

Many years later, on the outbreak of World War II, his son joined the RAF as a fighter pilot. He died in combat over the fields of Kent at the age of 26, and is buried alongside his father on the hillside overlooking Parnham. Truly a sad case of history repeating itself.

The Escape of Charles II, if told in full, would fill a book. After being heavily defeated at Worcester he made his way secretly to Dorset with a price of £1,000 on his head - a very considerable sum in those days. Arrangements had been made for a Charmouth fisherman, Stephen Limbrey, to take an "eloping" couple to France, and Charles was to travel with them as their servant. His loyal companions in this venture were Lord Wilmot and Juliana Coningsby, and they would certainly have been executed if they had been captured by Cromwell's men. The three of them stayed at the Queen's Arms in Charmouth - their plan being to put to sea shortly after midnight.

Limbrey's wife, suspecting what was afoot, and fearing for his safety, prevented him from leaving his cottage. Some say she hid his trousers!

Their escape plan ruined, the fugitives headed on to Bridport with Charles acting the part of groom to Miss Coningsby, who rode behind him. After narrowly avoiding detection in Bridport, which was swarming with Roundhead troops, they escaped up Lee Lane on the eastern outskirts of the town. By devious means they then made their way over Gerrard's Hill along the route described in this walk, and so to Broadwindsor where they put up for the night at an inn. Shortly after their arrival a company of Roundhead troopers also arrived at the inn, and discovery seemed certain.

They were saved at the last second when a heated dispute arose between the officers and some of the villagers. Apparently one of the camp followers had just given birth to a baby, and the locals were determined that the offspring should not be left behind by the troops as a charge on their parish. The officers left the inn to settle the dispute, and Charles and his party hurriedly took this opportunity to continue their journey to Colonel Wyndham's manor house at Trent, near Sherborne. Needless to say, that was not the end of their adventures, but eventually Charles reached Shoreham, in Sussex, and made good his escape to France in a coal brig.

Walk 11

CHESIL BEACH AND AN ANCIENT RIDGEWAY

Abbotsbury Beach - St Catherine's Chapel - Abbotsbury village - Wears Hill - Abbotsbury Castle - Limekiln Hill - West Bexington - Abbotsbury Beach
Distance: Approx 9½ miles
O.S. Map: Pathfinder 1331 (1:25000); or 194 (1:50000)

I SUGGEST you allow at least four to five hours for this walk, choosing a fine, clear day in order to enjoy the magnificent coastal and inland views. There are several possible starting points along its circular route, but for this itinerary we begin at the car park immediately behind the Chesil Beach near Abbotsbury. It has the advantage that all your climbing comes early in the walk, after which it is mostly downhill or level walking.

On leaving the car park, turn left along a shingly track which runs immediately behind the beach. Pass through a waymarked hunting gate, keeping a tamarisk hedge on your left. On rounding a bend in the track you are confronted by an impressive skyline view of St Catherine's Chapel, whilst on your left you have a steep grassy hillside encircled by lynchets.

When you come to a three-armed fingerpost turn right on to the path marked: "Coast Path - Swannery". The path is clearly defined, and provides fine elevated views of the Fleet and Swannery on your right. Shortly after passing a small World War II blockhouse you will come to a waymark stone at the intersection of three footpaths. Here you turn left along a permissive footpath, which leads you up a steep grassy hillside. Pass close to the corner of the wood on your right, then continue roughly

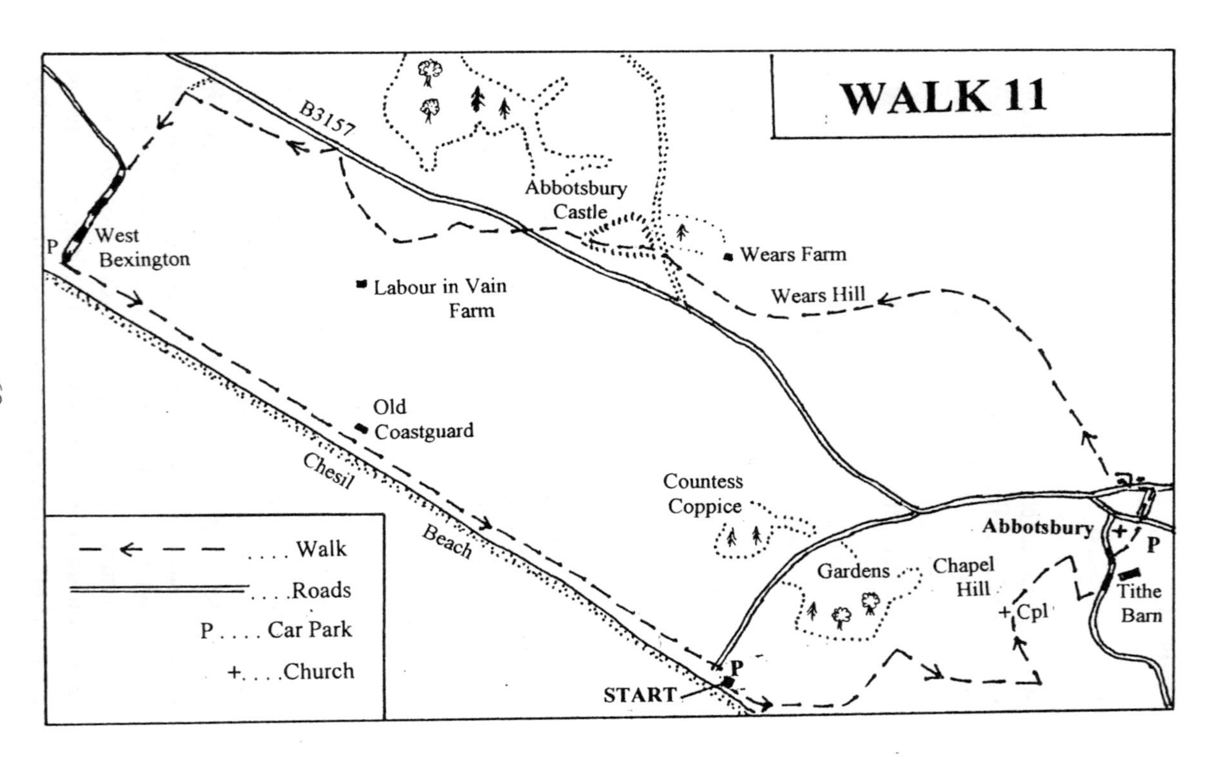
WALK 11
B3157
P
West Bexington
Abbotsbury Castle
Wears Farm
Wears Hill
Labour in Vain Farm
Old Coastguard
Chesil
Beach
Countess Coppice
Abbotsbury
P
Gardens
Chapel Hill
Cpl
Tithe Barn
P
START
Walk
Roads
P . . . . Car Park
+ . . . . Church

NNW. As you near the summit of the hill you will see St Catherine's Chapel ahead of you. (See **Points of Interest).** Access can usually be gained to the interior by a door on the N side.

On leaving the chapel head NE downhill along the main access track. While walking this stretch you are treated to a fine panoramic view of Abbotsbury village, with the church tower rising above the thatched roofs of golden-hued stone cottages. A little to the S of the village you will see the great 14th century thatched tithe barn. The rather strange-looking building standing alone beyond the barn is a medieval pigeon loft.

Near the foot of St Catherine's Hill you come to a group of farm buildings marked on the map as Furlong's Homestead. Alongside these buildings is another iron kissing gate. DO NOT go through this gate; instead do a sharp U-turn to your right and head S down a very pleasant grassy track, bordered on its left by a wall which once formed the western precinct of the now-vanished abbey.

Before long the path leads you over two stiles. The second stile brings you out on to a tarred lane, where you turn left and head uphill to the tithe barn and nearby duck pond, which together form a picture guaranteed to delight any camera-toting walker. The barn is now a museum of local rural bygones.

From here head on along the road for a few yards to the far side of the pond, where you will see a sign which reads: "To the Car Park". Take the indicated path and, after walking through the car park, cross the adjoining road and head up the tarred lane immediately facing you. Turn left when you reach a T-junction. After a few yards you will see, on your right, a narrow earth-surfaced lane alongside a thatched cottage. Head uphill along this lane, which after a couple of bends to left and right, sets off for the high downs to the N of Abbotsbury. After passing through a waymarked gate you soon come to a fingerpost alongside a water trough. The fingerpost indicates a track to "Lime Kiln Car Park". IGNORE this route and continue straight on along another unmarked track, still climbing towards a gate visible near the skyline.

Pass through this gate, which is waymarked, and continue uphill and through another field gate. Now bear diagonally left (NW) up a track which makes its way through a "notch" flanked by a limestone outcrop in the hillside. After passing this rocky outcrop you will see ahead another fingerpost clearly visible on the skyline. On reaching this, bear left on to the signposted path leading to "West Bexington".

This takes you over a stile and then straight on, keeping a wire fence on your right. You are now on a ridge-top track and it is all level grassy walking for some considerable distance, with only the buzzards and skylarks for company. This ridgeway has been in use since prehistoric times, and is dotted along its length by numerous tumuli. You also pass, as a matter of interest, the remains of a stone-built wartime lookout post, with a nearby manhole giving access to a deep, claustrophobic underground chamber where the lookout personnel used to sleep between watches. There is still the rusty remains of a bed down there!

Before long you cross a narrow lane and climb a bank leading into the turf-covered ramparts of an Iron Age hillfort popularly known as Abbotsbury Castle. The south-facing ramparts make an excellent spot to pause for a picnic lunch, providing at the same time some magnificent views of the surrounding coastline, from Portland Bill in the E to Golden Cap and Lyme Rgis at the W extremity of Dorset. On a clear day the view extends on around the South Devon coast as far as Start Point, some 60 miles distant as the gull flies.

You now head on towards the W extremity of Abbotsbury Castle. This part of the hilltop, where the ramparts converge, was later used by the Romans as a fort. If you look due W from this point you will see two gates, one on either side of the Abbotsbury to Bridport road. Descend the hillside to these gates and cross the road, keeping a wary eye open for fast-moving traffic. Here a National Trust sign reads: "Tulk's Hill".

Continue W over short rabbit-nibbled turf, keeping a stone wall on your left. Where the wall ends there is a fingerpost; continue W along the track marked: "West Bexington 1 mile". Before long you come to another fingerpost, and this time you follow the arm marked: "Coast Path". This brings you to yet another fingerpost quite nearby, and here you bear right, keeping a belt of scrubby, wind-stunted trees and brambles on your left. Before long you come to what is an unusual sight nowadays - a newly-built drystone wall. When I passed this way the stone looked as if it had been very recently quarried.

A waymarked stile leads over this wall and brings you on to a grassy path which runs between thickets of thorn trees. On emerging from this thicket the path heads mainly NW and brings you to the ruins of an old lime kiln. The kiln is fenced for reasons of safety, but a stile enables you to view it more closely - after which your path continues NW and before long brings you out on to the Bridport-Abbotsbury road. Immediately afterwards, however, you turn left off the road again on to another track signposted: "West Bexington ½ mile".

This track soon joins a narrow stone-surfaced lane.

Head down this lane, which was probably the old access route to the now vanished medieval village. (See **Points of Interest**). Today the lane is mostly grass-grown, and flanked by blackthorns and brambles.

Eventually you emerge on to a tarred road near the top end of West Bexington. Turn left, passing the Manor Hotel - or possibly pausing for one of their cream teas! After a short distance the road ends at the beach, and here you turn left and follow a track which heads E immediately behind the beach. At first the surface consists of soft scrunchy shingle, but soon the going becomes firmer and provides very pleasant walking. Eventually the track brings you back to your parked car.

Points of Interest

West Bexington. Apart from the Manor Hotel (originally a farm of some antiquity), present-day Bexington consists of a string of modern bungalows sited either side of the road leading to the beach. When I first visited this bit of coast, back in the 1930's, the land between beach and farm was almost deserted.

However, when the Domesday Book was compiled "Bessintone" was a fair-sized settlement, and had been in existence since Saxon times. It is recorded that around 1440 the village was attacked by French pirates, who burned down the dwellings and carried off the inhabitants. They were held to ransom, and although eventually redeemed for a large sum, the village was never rebuilt, and its site became farm land. An aerial photograph, taken by the RAF in 1948, clearly shows the grassed-over mounds of the lost village sited on the E side of the road, between the Manor Hotel and the beach.

Abbotsbury Church. Your walk takes you close to the parish church of St Nicholas, and a visit is well worthwhile. Just outside the porch are two ancient stone coffins, each with a recess for the occupant's head, and propped up inside the porch is a stone coffin lid, carved with the figure of an abbot holding a book and his pastoral staff. These relics almost certainly date back to the days of the great Benedictine abbey, which was founded during the reign of King Canute - and destroyed some 500 years later when Henry VIII ordered the dissolution of the monasteries.

The church contains many interesting links with Abbotsbury's eventful past, but possibly the most dramatic are two bullet holes in the Jacobean oak canopied pulpit. These are relics of the Civil War, when fighting took place in the church as a preliminary to the storming of adjoining Abbotsbury House, which was held for the king by Sir John Strangways.

The small group of Royalists inside the church, totalling 13 men, were soon overpowered and taken prisoner, but the seige of the manor house, built on the site of the old abbey, proved a tougher proposition.

Eventually, after six hours of fighting, the house was set ablaze and its occupants were forced to surrender. Whereupon a number of the victorious besiegers dashed into the blazing building to plunder its valuables. While they were inside the fire reached the gunpowder store, and the looters were blown up along with the house.

St Catherine's Chapel was built on its hilltop site by the abbey monks around the late 14th century, and it was used as a chantry for sailors, as well as providing them with a useful landmark. It is believed that a beacon fire may have been maintained on top of the tower. Buttressed, and with walls four feet thick, it is notable for the fact that it is constructed entirely of stone - no timber being used even in its roof.

Walk No. 12

IN SEARCH OF THE "MELBURYS"

Evershot - Melbury Park - Banger's Moor - Hazel Wood - Bubb Down - Melbury Bubb - St Edwold's Church - Chetnole Lodge - Melbury Sampford - Evershot
Distance: Approx. 7 miles
O.S. Map: Pathfinder 1298 (1:25000); or 194 (1:50000)

NOTE: I suggest that you carry binoculars on this walk. Among other things, Melbury Park contains several herds of deer, including red, fallow and Japanese Sika. They are usually most active during the rutting season - from late September and through October.

* * * * *

THIS interesting and rather unusual walk begins at the NE end of Evershot village. Here, on the N side of the road, in front of a picturesque cottage, you will see a large Lucombe oak tree spreading its branches over a triangular plot of grass. (See **Points of Interest**), Here a private road forks off into the grounds of Melbury Park. There is space to park just outside the entrance to the estate.

Set off along the tarred estate road, but after about 200 yards take the first turn off to your right (NE) along an unsurfaced lane that is classified as a public footpath. I mention this fact because walkers are required to keep to the authorised footpaths.

As we walked up this lane we met a keeper, whose two dogs were busy chivvying some over-adventurous pheasants out of the hedgerows, where they had been scratching for seeds and grubs. The birds were obviously used to the dogs, because they made no attempt to take

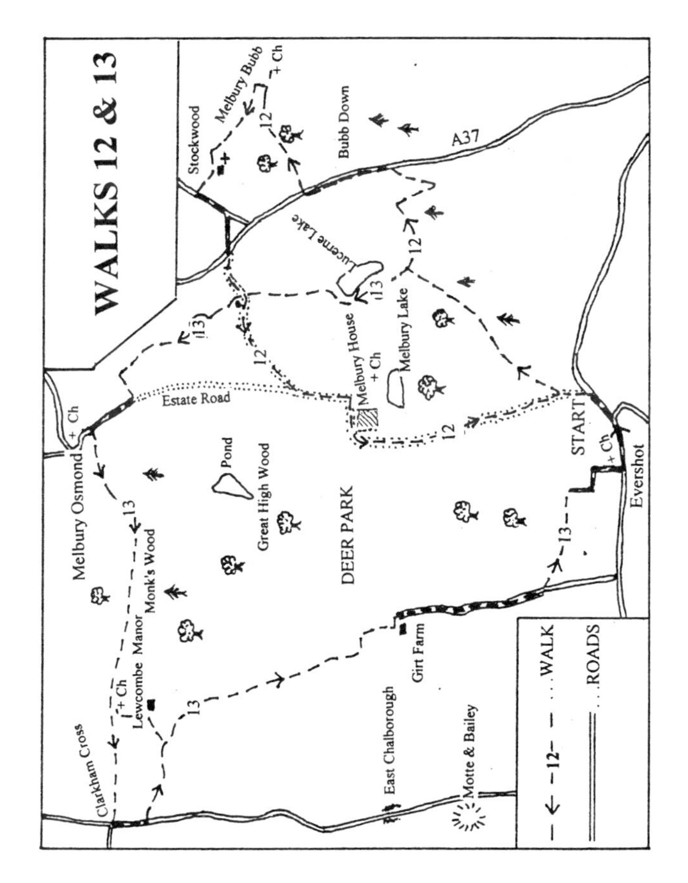

wing, but merely scuttled off like small boys caught scrumping in a forbidden orchard.

After about ½-mile you will arrive at a T-fork in the lane. Take the right-hand fork marked "Bridleway to the A37". This is a pleasant track which curves around through scattered woodlands, and then up through some pasture fields towards the main road. When the track forks at the edge of a recently planted wood take the right fork which is signed "Permissive bridleway". Head along this for about 200 yards until you come to a hard surfaced estate road curving around in a U-bend to your left, and then heading uphill.

This brings you to an exit on to the A37. Turn left along the broad grass verge for about 400 yards towards a layby - the "P" for parking sign is visible in the distance. Just beyond this layby you cross the road and head up an unsurfaced bridleway, with a wood on your left.

At the time of writing this bridleway was not waymarked, and it is not always easy to follow as there are several side-paths forking off to left and right. However, steering a course which varies between E and NE, and keeping to the high ground, it will not be long before you see Melbury Bubb village and church in the valley below. Keeping to the high ground, follow a line of stately beech trees, keeping them close on your right until you come to an iron gate. Turn right through this gate and then bear left downhill. After passing through two more gates, the path brings you out beside a farmhouse which was originally an Elizabethan manor house. Nearby Melbury Bubb church is well worth a visit. (See under **Points of Interest**).

After visiting the church you leave Melbury Bubb by your approach route, passing through the three gates previously mentioned. After passing through the third gate you head roughly NW. It is impossible to give clearer directions than this as there are no waymarks and no visible path - the right of way being over downland turf. Your best bet would be to keep any woodlands close on your right, but ignoring any gateways leading off into the woods.

Before long you come to a small but very steep grassy coombe in the hillside. Go down and up the far side of this coombe, and then, still keeping a fence on your right, you come very soon to a waymarked gateway and stile. Turn right over this and follow a footpath which winds its way through a dense hazel coppice.

Emerging from the coppice, you pick your way through a very muddy gateway, then cross some rough pasture land and approach a farmhouse. Here, alongside the house, you come upon St Edwold's church - one of the smallest in England, and the only one dedicated to this saint. His brother, Edmund, was king of East Anglia in the 10th century.

The church was open when I walked this way, and access was by a small brick footbridge over a stream. (See **Points of Interest**).

On leaving the church you continue the walk along the farm access road and then turn left on reaching the tarred county road. After about 300 yards follow the road around a sharp right-hand bend to the nearby A37.

Cross the A37 on to an estate road which you will see almost directly opposite. Follow this road over a cattle grid and past Chetnole Lodge into a tree-dotted expanse of parkland.

Before long, across the ranch-fenced paddocks on your left, you will see Melbury House. When the road you are travelling joins another at a T-junction, take the left turning, heading almost directly towards Melbury House. Follow the estate road around to the right, and then after crossing another cattle grid, keep a lookout for the herds of deer which roam the parkland away over on your right.

You leave the park by Lion Gate. In fact, there is no longer a gate here, although two imposing gate pillars remain, surmounted by a pair of stone lions. From here it is only a few more yards to your parked car.

Points of Interest

Melbury Bubb Church contains much of interest, and some of the stained glass in the windows dates back to 1474, when an even earlier church was rebuilt. On the N side of the nave, look for the four tracery lights which illustrate the parable of the Wise and Foolish Virgins. The foolish virgins are shown holding their lamps upside down.

Of special interest, however, is the font. It is intricately carved with what appears to be a hunting scene - the odd thing being that all the animals of the chase are upside down! Its origins are lost in antiquity, but there are theories aplenty. It used to be said that it once formed part of a pillar discovered in Norman times among the remains of a Roman villa. However, modern thinking suggests that it was more likely to have been the base of an early 11th century Anglo-Saxon carved cross, which was adapted by the Normans to provide a font.

St Edwold's Church, Stockwood. An information sheet in this unique little church tells us that Edwold was the younger brother of St Edmund, an Anglian king who was murdered by the Danes at the age of 30 in 870 AD. Heartbroken by his brother's death, Edwold refused the crown and left East Anglia. Eventually he settled near a spring at Cerne named Silver Well, but sadly he lived only a single year in Dorset and was buried at Cerne. Stockwood's earlier name was Stoke St Edwold, which has led many to surmise that Edwold had a cell here as well as at Cerne.

Melbury House. Much of this impressive house dates back to the 16th century. The estate was acquired by Henry Strangways in 1500, and his son, Sir Giles the elder, had already built extensively by 1540. The most noticeable feature of this early part of the house is its lantern tower, which can be glimpsed during the walk. The interior of the house is not open to the public, but the gardens and private church are occasionally opened for public viewing in aid of various charities.

The house is the home of Charlotte Townshend, one of Britain's richest women. Her various properties include the Ilchester Estate, Abbotsbury (including the famous Swannery) and part of the wealthy Holland Park area of London. After her marriage, in 1995, to James Townshend, Melbury House was the setting for a lavish ball with 650 guests. The festivities included a spectacular fireworks display set to music.

The Lucombe Oak. This distinctive hybrid evergreen oak tree is named after the Exeter nurseryman who first propagated it in the 1760's. It was around that time that Mr Lucombe discovered that this variety of oak could be raised when a Turkey oak and cork oak were grown in close proximity. Among the many seedling trees grown from the parent Turkey oak he noticed one that had the evergreen qualities of the cork oak, and by taking grafts from this tree on to ordinary Turkey oaks, and by other selective methods extending over many years, he succeeded in raising considerable numbers of the Lucombe oak, as it eventually came to be called. These were sold as young trees to many estates and landowners in the West Country, and one of them is the fine specimen you see here.

However, that is not the end of the story. During his lifetime Mr Lucombe felled the original oak that had brought him fame, and he then had the timber sawn up into boards for his own coffin. These he stored under his bed for safety, and there they were destined to remain for many years because he lived to the ripe old age of 102!

Walk No. 13

LEWCOMBE MANOR AND GIRT FARM

Evershot - Melbury Park - Lucerne Lake - Melbury Osmond - Lewcombe Manor - Girt Farm - Evershot
Distance: Approx. 7½ miles
O.S. Map: Pathfinder (1:25000); or 194 (1:50000)
NOTE: This walk begins and ends at the same parking spot as the previous one, and for the first mile or so it follows the same route. After that it branches off and explores a completely different type of countryside. You are almost certain to see plenty of wildlife, including deer and buzzards, and it is recommended that you carry binoculars.

However, it is inadvisable to attempt this walk within two days of a period of prolonged heavy rain, because at one point you will have to ford a small stream via some stepping stones. Under normal conditions a pair of well-waxed walking boots will keep your feet dry, but when in spate this little stream can become quite deep.

* * * * * *

Follow the directions given in Walk 12 until, after about a mile, you come to the T-junction. Here you turn LEFT (not right as in the previous walk). A belt of trees extends alongside the track, but before long you come to a gap in the trees which offers you a tree-framed glimpse of picturesque Lucerne Lake. On it we noticed a variety of waterfowl - including, rather surprisingly, a pair of cormorants.

Only a few yards beyond this viewpoint the track divides. Follow the right-hand (NE) track, which is waymarked with a Public Footpath notice and an arrow. This soon takes you through a gate and over a small bridge into a pasture field. Your path now heads N, keeping a wire fence and line of trees on your right.

Soon you come to a hunting gate. Pass through this and immediately turn left. You now find yourself on a rough track which becomes very muddy in wet weather. Continue straight on across a tarred estate road on to a continuation of your track, which after a few yards leaves the mud behind and becomes a very pleasant tree-bordered green lane.

At the end of this lane you pass through a five-barred gate and continue across the corner of a pasture field towards a hunting gate set in the hedge immediately opposite. This takes you into another green lane, which after a little while dives through a ford alongside a boisterous mini-waterfall. However, there is no need to get your feet wet here because, almost hidden in the overhanging foliage on your left, there is a recently built footbridge.

After crossing the bridge you carry on along a semi-sunken lane which burrows its way beneath rampant over-arching hazels, and then dips under a tunnel-like bridge. After emerging from the tunnel, turn sharp left and continue along a narrow path with banks on either side. Before long this brings you out on to a tarred road among a cluster of picturesque stone cottages. This is, in fact, the S end of Melbury Osmond - this part of the village being known as Town's End.

Turn right and head N along the tarred road. Before long you will see on your right a cottage with an unusual turreted corner. The next cottage to this is called "Rock Cottage", and immediately opposite this you turn left up a narrow lane, which soon becomes a dirt-surfaced track. Carry straight on until, after a mile or so, you come to a crossing of trackways. On a gatepost immediately facing you there is a blue bridleway waymark. Continue past this into a grassy field, keeping a wood close on your left. At the far left-hand corner of this field you will come to a waymarked iron hunting gate. Go through this gate, and then follow the path round to the right.

This rough but well-defined path leads you through a very pleasant wood. Soon you emerge very briefly into a rough grassy area, where a waymark on your left guides you straight ahead (W) into another wooded area. Head up a short slope and through another hunting gate into a large grassy field. Continue due W, keeping a hedge close on your right. At the far right corner of this field you will see a green iron gate, and this leads you on to a narrow track. On your left is a wood which changes at frequent intervals from hazel coppice to conifers, with here and there a batch of mature oaks and ash for added variety. The path climbs steadily, widening out into a very pleasant green lane, and eventually brings you out on to a tarred road at signposted Clarkham Cross.

Turn left along this road for a little way until you come to the entrance to Lewcombe Manor. Turn left over a cattle grid on to the estate road, which is classified as a bridleway. Soon, some little distance away to your right, you will see a house, newly built in yellowish stone. Ignore this house, and continue along the drive until you come to a second house close on your right. Skirt the hedged garden of this house, and round the corner on your right you will see a waymarked gate. (NOTE: The main route for this walk lies through this gate, as described in the next paragraph. However, a short diversion can be made by continuing along the bridleway, bearing left around the rear of Lewcombe Manor house to the tiny church nearby. Return to this gate by the same route.)

Pass through the waymarked gate and head across a grassy field in a SE direction; then go through a green-painted iron gate into another pasture field.

Head downhill across this field in a roughly SSE direction and you will soon see a rather dilapidated hunting gate giving access into a wood. IGNORE this gate, and instead follow the neighbouring hedge along to your right. Round a sharp bend in the hedge you will come to a stile. On crossing this stile you will come to a stream which you cross on stepping stones. (Even in dry weather these stones have very little freeboard!) The ascent up the opposite bank of the stream is quite steep, but fortunately a tree growing on the bank provides, with its roots, some useful steps.

This brings you out into another pasture field. Head SSE towards the far left-hand corner. After breasting a rise in the centre of the field you will see an iron gate with a stile alongside. Cross this and continue along the same heading to another gate. The land immediately to the left of this section of the walk is a deer park, and from several vantage points you are likely to see herds of fallow, red and sika deer. During the rutting season (October) you are also likely to hear the almost lion-like roaring of the bucks.

Many buzzards were also in evidence when we walked this path, whilst over to the right the abrupt upthrust of Castle Hill, near East Chelborough, provided another point of interest. It was once the site of a medieval stronghold, and the turf-covered motte and bailey help to give the hill a most distinctive appearance.

Still heading roughly SSE, you pass through two more gates which lead you across grassy fields and then on to a rough track. To your right you soon see the outbuildings of Girt Farm - the word "girt" being West Country dialect for "big" or "great". When we walked this way there was certainly a girt muck-spreading operation in progress, with a veritable fleet of muck-spreaders being filled up at a slurry pit by a JCB. Our right of way appeared to run directly beneath the slurry-slavering maw of this machine, but to our relief a waymarked turn-off to the left diverted us in the nick of time around the right-hand edge of a grassy patch, and through a gate at the top right-hand corner.

On emerging from the gate you now head due S on to a tarred farm road known as Girt Lane. This lane climbs steadily all the time, and as you gain height the views behind you become more and more impressive. When we walked this way the farm-dappled slopes of the Mendip Hills were clearly visible in the low-lying October sun, whilst far beyond them the distance-purpled heights of the Brecon Beacons and Black Mountains etched the skyline, some 80 miles away in Wales.

Eventually, after cresting the hill, you will come to a waymarked stile in the left-hand hedge of the lane. Cross this stile into a pasture field and head roughly E, keeping the hedge on your left; pass through a gate and continue across the next field to a stile, where you turn right along a narrow lane which will lead you to Evershot village. Turn left along the village street, past the Acorn Inn, and so back to your starting point.

Points of Interest

Lucombe Oak. See under Walk No. 12.

Walk No. 14

BY BRIDLEWAY TO CORSCOMBE

Hore Stones - Urless Farm - Coombe Bottom - Beckham Coppice - Corscombe - Corscombe Church - Urless Farm - Hore Stones
Distance: Approx 5 miles
O.S. Map: Pathfinder 1298 (1:25000) or 194 (1:50000)

THIS interesting and varied wildtrack walk begins at a layby on the A356 between Crewkerne and Dorchester. The layby (map reference 518034) has an information board, and advance warning of one's approach to it is provided by brown roadside "Information" signs.

Before starting your walk you may like view the ancient Hore Stones (see **Points of Interest**) which are situated only a few yards away on a triangular grassy patch on the opposite side of the road.

Returning to the layby, continue NE along the road for just a few yards, then turn right down an unsignposted private lane (classified as a bridleway) leading to Urless Farm. Shortly before reaching this impressive-looking farmhouse the bridleway turns left through a field gate and heads NNE up a grassy hillside, keeping to the left of a group of trees. On your right you will see a picturesque lake.

After reaching the group of trees, bear round to your right and follow a reasonably distinct track through another iron gate. From here you continue approximately NNE, and this will soon bring you to a line of trees. Keep these trees on your left, and before long you'll come to a small hunting gate. Pass through this gate, still heading NNE. This will bring you on to a steep, grassy hillside which (at the time of writing) has been recently planted with young trees. Continue along the contour line of the hillside, still keeping the trees on your left, and soon this will bring you to another hunting gate leading into an old wood. At first there is only a faint track to mark the bridleway, although some saw cuts in two fallen trees indicates where some attempt has been made to clear the path of obstructions. However, before long, heading downhill, you suddenly enter a wide ride.

On reaching the other side of the wood you emerge into a grassy field through another hunting gate. Here you turn left (W), keeping the perimeter of the wood on your left. This will bring you to a hunting gate waymarked with a blue bridleway arrow. You will now see ahead of you a steep-sided coombe. The bridleway is now barely discernible, but you should climb diagonally up the right-hand flank of the coombe towards the skyline.

On reaching the fence which runs along the skyline, you pass through a gateway and head diagonally left across this next field (roughly SW) and in the far hedge you will come to a green-painted hunting gate. This leads you across a tarred road and, directly opposite, through another larger gate into a pasture field. Incidentally, both these gates are waymarked, but as the waymark discs are nailed horizontally to the top of the gateposts you can easily overlook them. Also, the arrow on the second waymarked gate points too far to the left, so you should ignore it and instead head NNE towards another distant hunting gate.

Continue on the same heading through this gate until, near the bottom left-hand corner of the field, you come to another gate beneath some over-arching trees. The bridleway now becomes more distinct and after passing through another gate you continue straight on, ignoring a wider track curving off to the left towards some wooden chalets. Before long your path joins a narrow green lane hedged on either side with over-arching hazel bushes. Turn right along this lane. This takes you into Corscombe village, where you turn left for a few yards until, on your left, you come to a cream-washed cottage called Pitt's

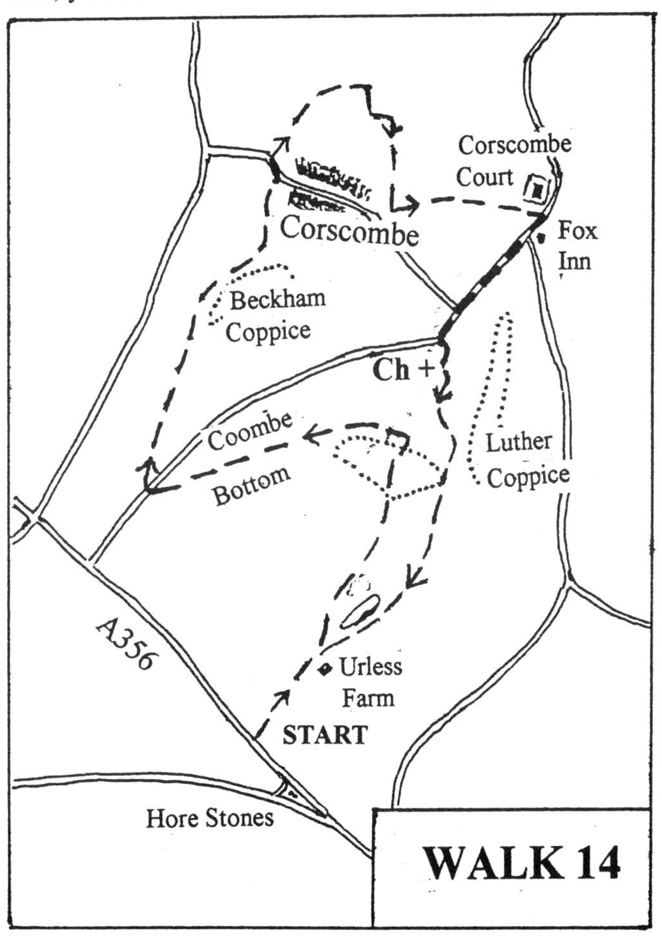

Farm. Immediately opposite you will see a small lane leading off to your right.

Head up this lane, which soon degenerates into an earth track, and continue until you come to a T-junction. Turn right here. After a few twists and turns, this lane brings you back to the eastern end of Corscombe village. However, just before the earth lane joins up with the tarred village street, look out for a gate in the left-hand hedge. Go through this gate into a grassy field, and follow a public footpath which runs downhill alongside the hedge on your right.

At the lower right-hand corner of this field you pass through another gate, and then turn sharp right (E). After a few yards the path crosses into a neighbouring arable field by a low stile which at the time of writing consists of little more than a bar of wood set a couple of feet above the ground. Continue E along the headland of this field; then pass through a gate on to a track which runs just S of moated Corscombe Court. (See **Points of Interest**).

You now emerge on to a tarred road. Turn right and after a few yards you pass (or pause at!) the picturesque Fox Inn, which looks out on to a pleasant expanse of grass complete with pigeon cote and several picnic tables. Continue straight on until you come to the left-hand turn-off to Corscombe Church. Turn down this lane, past the church and down a steepish hill. Near the foot of this hill the lane is bordered by a deep little stream-filled gorge.

Here you come upon an isolated cottage standing at the intersection of several bridleways and footpaths. Continue straight on, keeping the cottage on your right, and just a few yards beyond it you will see a waymarked gate under a large oak tree. Go through this gate into a pasture field and head roughly SSW, keeping a line of trees and a half-hidden stream close on your right.

Near the far bottom right-hand corner of this field you will come to an apology for a stile. It is a bar of timber laid along the top of a barbed wire fence, with no step to help you climb over. People with short legs should grit their teeth and think of England!

After negotiating this obstacle you keep a wire fence close on your right-hand side, following it around a sharp right-angle bend. After this you cross another stile, which brings you into an area of rough tussocky grass with a path running across it towards the edge of a wood.

On entering the wood all visible signs of the path virtually disappear. On your left rises a steep hillside, which falls away less steeply on your right. The best plan is to stick to the middle ground, climbing neither too high up the left-hand slope, nor allowing yourself to drift too far down to the right, where the terrain becomes increasingly boggy underfoot.

On reaching the far side of the wood you come to a wire fence. Turn right and follow this downhill until you come to an exit point which leads you out on to the bank of the lake you saw at the outset of this walk.

In spring and summer this lake is a favourite nesting place of wild fowl, so do not disturb them by lingering unnecessarily near the bank, or by causing any noise. Needless to say, dogs should be kept on a lead both here and in all the woodlands.

Soon the path, such as it is, curves around between the main lake and a smaller one on your left, and then passes through an iron gate. Bear left beyond this gate, and you now find yourself back near Urless Farm. From here you retrace your steps to your parked car.

Points of Interest

The Hore Stones, protected by a wooden rail fence, lie embedded in a triangular grassy "gore" where the main A356 is joined by a side road from Beaminster. Beneath the tarred surface of both these roads history lies in layers like the skin of an onion. Normans, Saxons, Romans and prehistoric tribesmen all used this ridgeway route, and it has been suggested that the Hore Stones served as Saxon boundary stones. Alternatively, being sited at a fork in the track, it seems possible that they may have been placed there even further back in time as a direction guide. That they are indeed very ancient is made obvious by the fact that they now lie in a shallow excavation, well below the surface of the modern road.

Corscombe Church stands on a hill some distance above the village, and as you pass it on your walk it is well worth a visit. The gargoyle-guarded porch, Tudor doorway and tower are all 15th century; the remainder was mostly rebuilt around 1875.

Corscombe Court is situated a short distance from the village, and originated in the 13th century as a farmstead built in a forest clearing. Although structurally altered over the years, the house, yard and outbuildings still retain their medieval farmstead layout, and all are clustered within a defensive moat, now partly filled in on two sides.

The farm was originally a grange of Sherborne Abbey, and the farm buildings include a fine 15th century tithe barn. Later in its history, in 1741, the manor was purchased by Thomas Hollis, whose outspoken democratic beliefs upset many of his well-to-do neighbours. As squire of Corscombe, he was always ready to help those in need, and this side of his character gained him the love and admiration of his workers and villagers. He contributed funds and books to many universities, including Harvard - a family tradition which had begun in 1690, and which his successors continued until 1804.

Thomas Hollis was a true eccentric, and one of his foibles was to give his fields and woods names which would perpetuate his beliefs . . . "Revolution", Republic", "Toleration", to name just a few. Glancing at the 1:25000 O.S. map, I see two other such names which would seem to bear his hallmark: Comprehension Coppice and Luther Coppice. No lover of royalty, local legend also has it that he called one batch of woodland "Stuart Coppice" so that every few years he would have the pleasure of seeing it "beheaded"!

He also had some very definite views on diet which must have seemed strange to those who knew him, although modern views on healthy eating now make them seem less peculiar. He took neither alcohol nor butter, milk, sugar or spices, and also avoided salt whenever possible.

During his adult life he never attended church, and on several occasions expressed the hope that he would be spared a lingering illness, and that when he died he would be buried in an unmarked grave, in one of the Dorset fields he loved so deeply. So when one day he suddenly collapsed and died while talking to some of his workmen in one of his fields, they buried him ten feet down and ploughed over the grave to conceal its whereabouts.

So spare Squire Hollis a brief thought as you enjoy this walk. He may be resting somewhere along your route. From all accounts he was a man who cherished the simple pleasures of life, so we can be sure he would welcome the passing tread of today's walker and country lover.

Also by Hugh Stoker:

SOUTH DORSET WALKS

A companion guide to twenty circular wildtrack walks between Abbotsbury and the Isle of Purbeck, including several in the heart of the "Hardy Country".

*   *   *   *   *

WEST DORSET WALKS

More of the author's favourite walks in West Dorset are described in this popular pocket guide. In print for over twenty years, it is still a best seller.

*   *   *   *   *

EAST DEVON WALKS

A similar guide which explores the superb stretch of country and coastline between the Exe Valley and the West Dorset border.